English as a
Second Language

Phase Two: Let's Read

English as a Second Language

Phase Two:
Let's Read

William Samelson

San Antonio College

RESTON PUBLISHING COMPANY, INC., Reston, Virginia 22090

A Prentice-Hall Company

Library of Congress Cataloging in Publication Data

Samelson, William, 1928-
    English as a second language, phase two: let's
read.

    Includes index.
    1. English language--Text-books for foreigners.
2. Readers--1950-   I. Title.
PE1128.S2175   428'.6'4   74-30253
ISBN 0-87909-258-0
ISBN 0-87909-257-2 pbk.

© 1975 by
RESTON PUBLISHING COMPANY, INC.
A Prentice-Hall Company
Box 547
Reston, Virginia 22090

10   9   8   7   6   5   4   3   2   1

Printed in the United States of America

For my parents, Harry and Bela,
in loving memory

Preface

LET'S READ, PHASE TWO is to be used as an introductory reader for students of English as a second language. The book is intended for a one-semester intensive course. We assume that the student has a basic knowledge of spoken English. This text aims at enlarging the student's passive (cognitive) vocabulary for better comprehension of written material. Hopefully, with intensive practice, passive comprehension will be converted into actively generated structures and ideas. This text reinforces structures already learned and introduces the student to different types of discourse: narrative, expository, and descriptive.

Our aim is, therefore, to provide the student with the ability to read independently and competently. To achieve the above objectives we undertake the following:

1. To combine sight and sound. Reading will be performed silently and verbally.
2. To identify word meaning in context rather than in isolation.
3. To heighten the student's ability to identify the meaning of complete phrases mechanically through rapid recognition.

LET'S READ is primarily aimed at the adult college student, whether native English-speaking with the need for remedial learning, or a native of a

vi

foreign country wishing to live or study in an English-speaking environment. However, by utilizing the context appropriately, the book may also be found useful for the instruction of students of high-school age.

One of the main advantages of this text is that its scope is limited. It is a basic language course with emphasis on *reading*. A sincere effort has been made here to simplify without oversimplification. In this endeavor, we have been guided by our desire to make language-learning easier than it is customarily experienced.

A few words about the format of the book are in order. LET'S READ is composed of ten chapters. These chapters should be taken up in sequence for maximum effectiveness. Each chapter is divided into ten sections, and each of the sections fulfills a specific function within the chapter. An attempt should, therefore, be made to complete each of the sections. However, the order and extent of coverage of these sections are left up to the discretion of the instructor. The section approach makes it possible for the instructor to determine the order of presentation of material best suited for the needs of his class.

I. NARRATIVE

Each narrative is an original composition dealing with everyday situations and containing everyday words and phrases. All narratives are arranged according to context, whether *concrete* or *abstract*. They range from stories of general interest to those of specific interest. These narratives are for the most part simple in form, with some degree of sophistication in later chapters. Finally, there exists a length variant.

The contextual presentation of the narratives is such that grammatical and syntactical structures become obvious. The structures presented in the initial narrative will recur in the following nine. What is learned is thus reinforced, eliminating the necessity of memorization.

II. WORDS IN CONTEXT (Pictograph)

The narrative is presented in a series of *pictographs*. Words used in the narrative are listed below each pictograph. Where possible, [synonyms] and (*antonyms*) are printed after each word.

In this manner, the student learns new words and expressions in their varied usage within the context of a narrative. He reconstructs the narrative using related words. This practice will improve the learner's reading speed and comprehension. It will also offer him a wider range of vocabulary.

III. STRUCTURES (Phrases)

The incomplete *phrases* are the smallest, disrupted fragments of the narrative. They are to be converted orally into complete sentences. The phrases are presented in the sequence in which they occur in the narrative.

IV. SENTENCES

In section iv the isolated phrases from section III have now become complete, but simple, *sentences*. The sentences are also presented in the sequence in which they occur in the narrative. They are to be read aloud. Substitution of related words for the italicized ones will make this exercise meaningful and not a mere rote performance.

V. GRAMMAR AND SYNTAX

In this section we attempt to satisfy the analytical mind of the student. There are complete paradigmatic sets where necessary in reference to the items learned. Grammatical structures offered here are presented within the framework of each narrative and should be orally identified. The teacher will find it helpful to devote a good portion of time to this section, for it will help the student to know the mechanics of the language in order to facilitate comprehension.

VI. WORD RECOGNITION

Words are selected from the narrative. The student is given the opportunity to identify the synonym (later the antonym) of each selection. This will contribute to building an active vocabulary. This section is to be used as a timed *diagnostic word test* in which the student defines each word studied in the narrative. New sentences may be constructed using the newly identified word.

VII. CONCEPT RECOGNITION

Concepts contained in the narrative are chronologically listed. They are to be studied with constant reference to word recognition. This chronological study serves to reinforce recognition of concept relations and mastering of grammatical order.

VIII. TELLING THE MEANING

This exercise is to be read orally. Complete sentences are to be constructed using words related in meaning to those given. This section should also be a timed *diagnostic word test.*

IX. COMPREHENSION (Exercises)

A variety of comprehensive exercises are presented, testing for word-recognition, idea-patterns, and the meaning of isolated material taken from the narrative. These may be used at the discretion of the instructor. The exercises serve a double purpose: (1) their abundance gives the instructor more latitude in the use of this text; (2) they enable the student to analyze the narrative independently. These exercises should be an enjoyable experience for both the student and teacher rather than an arbitrary work load.

X. DISCUSSION AND EVALUATION

This section of each chapter serves as a summary for both teacher and student. Having studied the preceding sections thoroughly, the student should now be ready to read and interpret the entire narrative. He should undertake to discuss the story in context and, if possible, relate other experiences of similar nature.

The *evaluation* part of this section is for review and evaluation of things learned, and is presented in the form of short quizzes.

Poetry is an integral part of a language and should be introduced early in the student's language-learning career. Poems are used here as a device for improving reading comprehension and for providing an outlet for simple literary analysis.

Finally, the author believes that one of the most exciting features of this text is that it gives the student time to achieve success. There is no necessity for "cramming" in order to complete the text, although frequent reviewing and testing are desirable to spot-check and reemphasize important points.

And now, wishing you success in the improvement of your reading habits, I would like to begin with the following *declarative* sentence followed by an *imperative* sentence.

This is a neat book. Read it!

* * *

William Samelson

Acknowledgements

Needless to say, I owe a debt of gratitude to many for their generous contributions to the preparation of this text: to such scholars as Jespersen, Politzer, Fries, Croft, and Dykstra who have influenced my thinking through their works; and to my colleagues, James Banford, Joseph Dunwoody, Jr., and Isabel Vera Cruz for their offer to use these lessons in experimental stages and for making various suggestions. Special thanks are due to my secretarial staff under the guidance of Lucinda Cabasos, who worked on the final draft of the manuscript. Finally, particular thanks go to my children for their understanding during my long hours of isolation, and to my wife Rosita who so ably helped to assuage these hours of crisis.

Introduction

A listing of some common grammatical terms is in order.

I. Parts of Speech

We recognize in every sentence, words that fulfill a specific function. Such words are called *parts of speech.* There are basically **eight** such words: (1) noun, (2), verb, (3) pronoun, (4) adjective, (5) adverb, (6) preposition, (7) conjunction, and (8) interjection.

A. **Noun**—means a person (*Abraham Lincoln*); place (*Illinois*); thing [animal or object] (*lion, book*); quality (*wisdom*); state (*honesty, sadness*); or action (*exercise, play*). A common marker of a noun is the determiner "the" or "a."

B. **Verb**—expresses action (*study, run*); state of being or condition (*be, is*).

C. **Pronoun**—takes the place of a noun phrase (*he, she, it, we, you, they*).

D. **Adjective**—modifies, describes, or limits the noun (*good* man, *bad* student; *many* things).

E. **Adverb**—modifies the verb (read *slowly*), adjective (*extremely* slow), or adverb (*very* quickly).

F. **Preposition**—shows the relationship between a noun or pronoun and another word (water *under* the bridge, think *before* speaking).

G. Conjunction—joins words or groups of words   (Rose *and* Bill, it's good to be poor in money *but* rich in spirit.)

H. Interjection—shows emotion (*Gosh!*, *Damn!*), an exclamation of surprise (*Oh! Gee!*), delight (*Wow! Hurrah!*), etc.

II. *The Sentence*

The sentence consists of a group of words that present a meaningful thought. It is classified according to its *use* or *function*. The sentence contains two main parts: noun phrase + verb phrase. There are five major types of sentences.

A. Declarative Sentence (Statement)
   He studies English. (Affirmative)
   He doesn't study English. (Negative)
B. Interrogative (Word Question) Sentence
   Why does he study English?
   Where does he study English?
C. Imperative (Command, Request) Sentence
   Give me the book!
   Study English!
D. Exclamatory Sentence (Expresses Emotion)
   What a nice day!

III. *The Paragraph*

There is no set rule for the number of words or sentences a paragraph must contain. The most common paragraph, however, links several related sentences. These sentences should focus on the same topic; they clarify, amplify, and defend it.

The following is a typical paragraph:

> *A topic sentence usually comes first in the paragraph. It contains the main idea of the paragraph. The rest of the paragraph consists of sentences which support the topic sentence. Some sentences refer directly to the topic sentence. Others may expand the ideas of the topic sentence.*

A road warning sign may serve as an illustration of a paragraph:

> *ATTENTION! THIS ROAD IS UNDER CONSTRUCTION. PROCEED WITH CAUTION. MEN AT WORK. SPEED LIMIT 20 MPH. THE LIFE YOU SAVE MAY BE YOUR OWN.*

An advertising poster may serve as an example of a short visual paragraph (**pictograph**):

IV. Key to Word Recognition

A. Some Common Prefixes and Roots

By knowing the meaning of prefixes, roots, and suffixes, and being able to combine them, one may often be able to determine the meaning of a word. The following are only a few examples of such word components. They are listed here in the hope that this knowledge will enable the student to learn a whole word family when learning a new word. For example, from the word *dramatize* we can learn *dramatization, dramatist, dramaturgy,* etc.

PREFIX	GENERAL MEANING	ROOT	GENERAL MEANING	EXAMPLE
circum-	around	*nav*	sail, ship	circumnavigate
de-	away from, down	*tain*	hold	detain
dis-	opposing, apart from not, off	*pos*	put, place	dispose
epi-	on, over, upon, near, beside	*gram* *graph*	writing	epigram epigraph
intro-	between, among	*duc*	lead	introduce
mal-	bad	*vol*	wish	malevolent
mis-	wrong	*anthrop*	man, mankind	misanthrope
over-	excessive, above	*dra*	do, act	overdramatize
pre-	before	*clude*	close, shut	preclude
sub-	under, below beneath	*vers* *vert*	turn	subvert
syn-	with, together	*onym*	name	synonym
trans-	beyond, over across	*fus*	pour	transfusion
uni- *mono-*	one, alone	*form* *gamy*	shape marriage	uniform monogamy

Contents

Chapter One

Friends Meet

I.   *Narrative*

A.   It is an early morning class. The students assemble in the classroom. They wait for their teacher, Mr. Preston. He is late for class. He is delayed on his way to school because there is a traffic jam on the freeway.

B.   Mr. Preston arrives five minutes later. The students are eager to begin their lesson. They study English. The students need to learn the language of the land. They come from many parts of the world, and they don't know each other by name. Mr. Preston tells the students to stand up as they tell their names.

C.   There are Gail Phillips and Arthur Jones. They are new Americans. There is also Marcel Boileau. Marcel comes from Paris, France. Gail thinks Marcel has a funny name. The students laugh. They are unable to pronounce his name the way he does. Marcel is glad to be in the United States.

D.   Marcel has many relatives in France. He visits them during vacation. He likes his American friends. Some of his classmates plan their vacations early. They all like to travel.

E.   Mr. Preston shows some places on the map of America. Marcel points out places to visit on the map of France. The lesson is interesting, and all students get acquainted.

F.   After the lesson, the students go to the cafeteria. They meet there often after classes. It has a relaxed atmosphere. They talk while they eat. Some students don't talk. They just listen. You can learn about many things when you listen well. They talk about customs. People have different customs, but they are friendly. Marcel likes his friends.

* * *

II.   *Words in Context   [Pictographs]*

Below are some of the words used in the narrative. Where possible, each word has a [synonym], or it is defined as used in the story. Where possible, an (*antonym*) is also given. Make up sentences about the pictographs choosing the words you need. Read aloud.

Example: [**group of students**] = There is a group of students.

A. B. and C.

morning [**early in the day**] (*evening*); class [**group of students**]; assemble [**gather**]; teacher [**instructor**]; delay [**detain**]; freeway [**expressway**] classroom [**schoolroom**]; eager [**anxious**]; need [**want**]; begin [**start**] (*finish*); part [**section**]; stand up [**get up**]; know [**be acquainted with**]; come [**arrive**] (*leave*); think [**reason**]; funny [**strange**] (*serious*); laugh [chuckle] (*cry*); to be unable [cannot]; pronounce [articulate]; glad [happy] (*sad*)

Drawing of paragraph A, B & C in Dialogue

D. E. and F.

many [a lot of] (*few*); relative [family]; vacation [rest] (*work*); like [fond of] (*dislike*); friend [ally] (*enemy*); classmate [fellow student]; travel [journey]; place [locality]; show [point out]; interesting [fascinating]; get acquainted with [meet]; often [frequently] (*seldom*); relaxed [comfortable]; atmosphere [feeling]; listen [hear]; friendly [amicable]

III. Structures [Phrases]

Below are some *phrases* taken from the narrative. Make complete sentences and read them aloud.

Drawing of paragraph D, E & F

A.	morning	—	class		
B.	assemble	—	in	—	the classroom
C.	for	—	their	—	teacher
D.	late	—	for	—	class
E.	on	—	his	—	way
F.	on	—	the	—	freeway
G.	begin	—	lesson		
H.	need	—	to	—	learn
I.	of	—	the	—	land
J.	from	—	many parts		
K.	of	—	the	—	world
L.	to	—	stand up		
M.	they	—	tell	—	names
N.	has	—	funny	—	name
O.	to	—	pronounce		
P.	way	—	he	—	does
Q.	glad	—	to	—	be

R.	some	—	of	—	classmates
S.	their	—	vacation	—	early
T.	places	—	to	—	visit
U.	after	—	the	—	lesson
V.	often	—	after	—	school
W.	while	—	they	—	eat
X.	because	—	you	—	listen
Y.	about	—	customs		
Z.	his	—	American	—	friends

IV. Sentences

A. Read the following sentences aloud. Repeat, substituting where possible, the synonym of the word in *italics*, or a phrase that explains the meaning. Make other necessary changes.

Example: It is a *class.*
It is a *group of students.*

1. The students *assemble.*
2. He is *delayed.*
3. Mr. Preston is on the *freeway.*
4. Mr. Preston *arrives.*
5. The students are *eager.*
6. They *don't know* each other.
7. Marcel has a *funny* name.
8. Marcel is *glad* to be in the United States.
9. He *likes* his friends.
10. Mr. Preston *shows* some places.
11. The lesson is *interesting.*

B. Fill in the following blanks with words from the narrative. Each space may be filled by a word or phrase. Do not refer back to the narrative. Where possible, use variations of the missing words. Read aloud.

It is an _____ morning _____ . The students _____ in the _____ . They _____ for their _____ . Mr. Preston is _____ for _____ . He is _____ on his _____ to school _____ there is a _____ on the _____ .

Mr. Preston _____ five _____ later. The _____ are _____ to _____ their lesson. They _____ English. They _____ from _____ parts of the _____ . The students don't _____ each other. The students _____ while they _____ their names.

Gail and Arthur are_____. Marcel_____from France. Marcel has a_____name. The students are_____to pronounce his name and they _____.

Marcel has_____in France. He_____them during_____. Some of his _____plan to_____France. The students _____ to _____. Mr. Preston_____the_____of America. Marcel_____out_____to visit in France. The lesson is _____ , and all _____ get _____.

After the_____ , the students_____to the_____. They_____there often_____classes. It is a_____atmosphere. Some students _____ _____. They just_____. You can _____ many things_____ you listen. Students talk_____customs. People_____different_____.

V. Grammar and Syntax   (Points of Interest)

A. **The Simple Present Tense** expresses PRESENT TIME, GENERAL ACTION, HABITUAL ACTION, and PRESENT CONDITION.

> The students *wait* for Mr. Preston.   (PRESENT TIME)
> He *is* late for class.   (PRESENT TIME)
> They *study* English.   (GENERAL ACTION)
> They *wait* for Mr. Preston each morning.   (HABITUAL ACTION)
> They *are* unable to pronounce his name.   (PRESENT CONDITION)
> Marcel *is* glad to be in the United States.   (PRESENT CONDITION)

- - - - - - - - - - - - - - - - - - - -

B. The **Personal Pronoun** refers to the

1. SPEAKER (the person(s) who speak(s)–*I* or *we*).
2. the PERSON SPOKEN to–*you.*

> *You* can learn about many things.

3. the PERSON or THING being SPOKEN of (*he, she, it, they*).

> *He* comes from France.
> *She* studies English.
> *It* is early.
> *They* all like to travel.

- - - - - - - - - - - - - - - - - - - -

C.   A **Declarative Sentence** makes, or denies, a statement. It has as its normal word order: the SUBJECT [Noun Phrase] and the PREDICATE [Verb Phrase]. The sentence ends with a period.

> They wait for Mr. Preston.
> The students study English.
> Marcel has relatives in France.
> His classmates plan their vacation.
> All students get acquainted.
> Marcel likes his friends.

D.   **Twelve** words have the function of **Noun Determiners.**
      They are: ARTICLES: *a, an, the*
                 POSSESSIVES: *my, your, our, his, their*
                 DEMONSTRATIVES: *this, that, these, those*

> He's *a* student.
> This is *an* early morning class.
> *The* teacher is delayed.
> *My* relatives live in France.
> They plan *their* vacation early.

Note: The **Non**definite article *a* is commonly used before words beginning with a consonant sound: *a* student, *a* relative, etc. *An* is used before words beginning with a vowel sound: *an* American, *an* early class, etc. There are some exceptions: *an* honor, *a* university, etc.

E.   The **Compound Sentence** has two or more full PREDICATIONS in the form of independent clauses. The clauses are frequently connected by words (CONJUNCTIONS) such as *and, but, for, nor, or, so, yet.*

> It is an early morning class *and* the students assemble.
> The teacher is late *for* there is a traffic jam.
> The students stand up *as* they tell their names.

VI.   *Word Recognition*

A.   Circle the word or phrase in Column II that is most *like* the word in Column I, and the word or phrase in Column III most *unlike* the word in Column I. This oral identification of words ought to be timed.

COLUMN I		COLUMN II		COLUMN III
1. **arrive**	a.	come	a.	leave
	b.	depart	b.	run
	c.	begin	c.	reach
2. **assemble**	a.	disperse	a.	show
	b.	gather	b.	point out
	c.	get to	c.	scatter
3. **be able**	a.	be capable	a.	be incapable
	b.	cannot	b.	can
	c.	be unable	c.	capable of
4. **begin**	a.	start	a.	stay
	b.	leave	b.	end
	c.	terminate	c.	continue
5. **come**	a.	study	a.	start
	b.	arrive	b.	commence
	c.	go	c.	leave
6. **different**	a.	distinct	a.	similar
	b.	new	b.	dissimilar
	c.	happy	c.	interesting
7. **eager**	a.	capable	a.	indifferent
	b.	competent	b.	lounging
	c.	anxious	c.	happy
8. **early**	a.	happily	a.	promptly
	b.	at an early hour	b.	late
	c.	eagerly	c.	unhappily
9. **funny**	a.	happy	a.	common
	b.	carefree	b.	withdrawn
	c.	strange	c.	unfriendly

10.	**glad**	a.	slow	a.	aware
		b.	happy	b.	sad
		c.	unusual	c.	unaware

11.	**interesting**	a.	serious	a.	slow
		b.	dull	b.	boring
		c.	fascinating	c.	fast

12.	**know**	a.	be acquainted with	a.	be unacquainted with
		b.	like	b.	be different
		c.	dislike	c.	like

13.	**laugh**	a.	understand	a.	take
		b.	chuckle	b.	give
		c.	hide	c.	cry

14.	**listen**	a.	hear	a.	dislike
		b.	study	b.	play
		c.	work	c.	ignore

15.	**morning**	a.	early in the day	a.	dawn
		b.	dusk	b.	evening
		c.	afternoon	c.	day

16.	**many**	a.	a lot of	a.	boring
		b.	fascinating	b.	numerous
		c.	happy	c.	few

17.	**often**	a.	once in a while	a.	seldom
		b.	sometimes	b.	never
		c.	frequently	c.	sometimes

18.	**relaxed**	a.	disagreeable	a.	sad
		b.	comfortable	b.	articulate
		c.	strange	c.	tense

19.	**stand up**	a.	get up	a.	sit
		b.	show up	b.	sit down
		c.	gather	c.	stand

B. In the space on the left write the word(s) that would best fit the expression(s) in **bold print**. Make other necessary changes. Read aloud.

_____ 1. The students **gather** in the classroom.

_____ 2. The teacher is **detained**.

_____ 3. Mr. Preston **comes** late.

_____ 4. There is a traffic jam on the **expressway**.

_____ 5. The students are **enthusiastic** to begin.

_____ 6. The lesson **starts** with new words.

_____ 7. They are all good **pupils**.

_____ 8. Mr. Preston is the **instructor**.

_____ 9. They come from many **sections** of the earth.

_____10. They **get up** to tell their names.

_____11. His name is **strange**.

_____12. Gail Phillips **chuckles** all the time.

_____13. Marcel is **happy** to have so many friends.

_____14. Marcel is **fond** of America.

_____15. They will **journey** together.

_____16. The teacher **points out** many places.

_____17. They find it **fascinating**.

_____18. Students **frequently** eat in the cafeteria.

_____19. They are **amicable** and respect the **different** customs.

VII. *Concept Recognition*

Fill in the word (phrase) most fitting to express the CONCEPT of the sentence according to the narrative. Read the complete sentence aloud.

A.   The students wait for their teacher because _____ .

    1. they like him   2. they have a class
    3. he is late   4. they study English

B. Mr. Preston is delayed on his way to school because _____ .

1. he cannot sleep
2. of a traffic jam
3. he forgets
4. his car breaks down

C. The students are eager to study English. They need to learn it because _____ .

1. English is funny
2. Mrs. Preston speaks English
3. it is the language of the land
4. Marcel learns it

D. They don't know each other by name because _____ .

1. they are not intelligent
2. they cannot pronounce
3. they live in France
4. they come from many sections of the world

E. To tell their names the students _____ .

1. sit down
2. laugh
3. stand up
4. are glad

F. Gail and Arthur study English because _____ .

1. they are glad
2. they study
3. they are able
4. they are new Americans

G. Because the students are not French, they cannot _____ .

1. pronounce Marcel's name
2. go to France
3. speak English
4. plan their vacation

H. Marcel goes to France to _____ .

1. see Mr. Preston
2. learn English
3. visit his relatives
4. eat at the cafeteria

I. His friends plan their vacation because they _____ .

1. like to travel
2. are students
3. see the map
4. like Marcel

J. While Mr. Preston points out places on the map, the students _____ .

1. laugh
2. think it is funny
3. are glad
4. get acquainted

K.   The students go to the cafeteria _____.

      1. to eat and talk   2. to look at the map
      3. to laugh   4. to learn the lesson

L.   The cafeteria has _____.

      1. many friends   2. maps
      3. a relaxed atmosphere   4. many students

M.   You learn about many things when you _____.

      1. listen well   2. speak English
      3. talk a lot   4. laugh

VIII.   *Telling the Meaning*

A.   Place a check mark (✓) in front of the word in Column II that best fits the MEANING of the word in Column I. Read aloud a complete sentence using this word.

COLUMN I   COLUMN II

1. **a lot of**   _____ a.   few
                                    _____ b.   many
                                    _____ c.   great

2. **be acquainted with**   _____ a.   know
                                    _____ b.   be ignorant of
                                    _____ c.   be good

3. **be fond of**   _____ a.   dislike
                                    _____ b.   correct
                                    _____ c.   like

4. **chuckle**   _____ a.   cry
                                    _____ b.   laugh
                                    _____ c.   run

5. **come**   _____ a.   arrive
                                    _____ b.   go
                                    _____ c.   depart

6. **competent**
   _____ a. able
   _____ b. funny
   _____ c. unable

7. **detain**
   _____ a. hasten
   _____ b. delay
   _____ c. block

8. **fascinating**
   _____ a. interesting
   _____ b. boring
   _____ c. intelligent

9. **frequently**
   _____ a. seldom
   _____ b. quickly
   _____ c. often

10. **gather**
    _____ a. scatter
    _____ b. come
    _____ c. assemble

11. **happy**
    _____ a. glad
    _____ b. sad
    _____ c. industrious

12. **hear**
    _____ a. listen
    _____ b. ignore
    _____ c. delay

13. **journey**
    _____ a. stay home
    _____ b. travel
    _____ c. leave

14. **start**
    _____ a. begin
    _____ b. end
    _____ c. know

15. **unlike**
    _____ a. same
    _____ b. different
    _____ c. unfriendly

B. Return to Exercise A. Place two check marks (✓✓) in front of the word in Column II that is the ANTONYM of the word in Column I. Read aloud a complete sentence using this word.

C. Select one of the three (3) words (phrases) that best fulfills the MEANING of the sentence according to the narrative. Insert the word in the blank space. Read the completed sentence aloud.

1. Students gather in the classroom＿＿＿＿ in the morning.
   a. early   b. late   c. enthusiastically

2. The teacher is delayed, and he is＿＿＿＿ for class.
   a. prompt   b. late   c. early

3. There is a traffic jam which＿＿＿＿ him.
   a. detains   b. hastens   c. waits

4. When Mr. Preston comes to class, the students are＿＿＿＿ to learn English.
   a. idle   b. eager   c. intelligent

5. To live in America, the students＿＿＿＿ to learn English.
   a. want   b. arrive   c. place

6. The students＿＿＿＿ and tell their names.
   a. sit down   b. get up   c. depart

7. Gail and Arthur are Americans, but Marcel＿＿＿＿ from Paris, France.
   a. goes   b. thinks   c. comes

8. Gail thinks Marcel has a＿＿＿＿ name.
   a. serious   b. able   c. strange

9. The students are＿＿＿＿ to pronounce the name.
   a. able   b. sad   c. unable

10. Marcel is＿＿＿＿ to be in the United States.
    a. sad   b. glad   c. envious

11. He is＿＿＿＿ his American friends.
    a. fond of   b. happy of   c. glad of

12. Mr. Preston and Marcel＿＿＿＿ some places on the map.
    a. hide   b. show   c. go

13. The places are＿＿＿＿ and the students are ＿＿＿＿ to visit them.
    a. fascinating, eager   b. boring, idle   c. serious, unable

14. After school the students_____ meet in the_____.
   a. seldom, school   b. frequently,   c. travel, home
                              restaurant

15. People have_____ , but they are_____ .
   a. same air, unfriendly   b. different customs,   c. tense world, keen
                                 friendly

IX. *Comprehension* *[Exercises]*

A.   Place a check mark (✓) in front of the correct answer to each of the questions according to the narrative. Do not consult the narrative. Read the complete sentence aloud.

1. When do the students meet for class?

   _____ a. When the teacher arrives.
   _____ b. Early in the morning.
   _____ c. When the time comes.

2. Who is late for class?

   _____ a. Mr. Preston is late for class.
   _____ b. The students are late for class.
   _____ c. Marcel is late for class.

3. Why is Mr. Preston delayed?

   _____ a. Because he waits for the students.
   _____ b. Because he cannot find the way.
   _____ c. Because there is a traffic jam on the freeway.

4. Where do the students come from?

   _____ a. They come from France.
   _____ b. They come from the United States.
   _____ c. They come from many parts of the world.

5. What does Mr. Preston tell the students?

   _____ a. He tells them to sit down.
   _____ b. He tells them to stand up.
   _____ c. He tells them to read.

6. What does Gail think about Marcel?

_____ a. She thinks he is sad.
_____ b. She thinks he has a funny name.
_____ c. She thinks he is serious.

7. Where does Mr. Preston point out places?

_____ a. He points them out on the map.
_____ b. He points them out in the book.
_____ c. He points them out in the cafeteria.

8. How is the lesson?

_____ a. The lesson is boring.
_____ b. The lesson is fascinating.
_____ c. The lesson is long.

9. Where do the students go after the lesson?

_____ a. They go to the cafeteria.
_____ b. They go home.
_____ c. They travel.

10. Why do the students meet in the cafeteria?

_____ a. They study.
_____ b. They laugh.
_____ c. Because it has a relaxed atmosphere.

11. What do the students do while they eat?

_____ a. They sing.
_____ b. They talk.
_____ c. They play.

12. Why do some students listen?

_____ a. Because they laugh.
_____ b. Because they think.
_____ c. Because they learn about things.

13. What do the students talk about?

_____ a. About English.
_____ b. About the United States.
_____ c. About customs.

14. What do people have?

    ____ a. They have different students.
    ____ b. They have different customs.
    ____ c. They have different friends.

B.   Below there are three (3) different thoughts expressed in each of the exercises. Assign the proper sequence (order) of THOUGHT, according to the narrative, by numbering 1 to 3. Read aloud.

1. a. the teacher   _____
   b. wait for   _____
   c. the students   _____

2. a. to begin their lesson   _____
   b. the students   _____
   c. are eager   _____

3. a. each other   _____
   b. they don't know   _____
   c. by name   _____

4. a. as they tell their names   _____
   b. Mr. Preston tells the students   _____
   c. to stand up   _____

5. a. Marcel has   _____
   b. Gail thinks   _____
   c. a funny name   _____

6. a. Marcel has   _____
   b. in France   _____
   c. many relatives   _____

7. a. to visit   _____
   b. Marcel points out places   _____
   c. on the map of France   _____

8. a. the students go   _____
   b. after the lesson   _____
   c. to the cafeteria   _____

9. a. you can learn   _____

    b. when you listen well   _____
    c. about many things   _____

10. a. people have   _____
    b. but they are friendly   _____
    c. different customs   _____

C.   There are some statements listed below about the narrative. Write **T** for **True** in front of each statement that you think is true. Write **F** for **False** if the statement is not true. Read aloud.

_____ 1. It is a late morning class.

_____ 2. The students wait for Mr. Preston.

_____ 3. The teacher is delayed.

_____ 4. A traffic jam detained him.

_____ 5. The students are eager about learning.

_____ 6. The teacher tells them to stand up.

_____ 7. They tell their names after they stand up.

_____ 8. Gail and Marcel are new Americans.

_____ 9. Gail thinks Marcel has a sad name.

_____ 10. The students are sad.

_____ 11. Marcel has relatives in France.

_____ 12. Marcel plans his vacation early.

_____ 13. Mr. Preston shows places on the map.

_____ 14. The lesson is fascinating.

_____ 15. The students eat and talk in the cafeteria.

_____ 16. There is a relaxed atmosphere in the cafeteria.

_____ 17. When you listen, you learn.

_____ 18. The students talk about customs.

_____ 19. People have the same customs.

_____ 20. People are friendly.

_____ 21. Marcel likes his friends in America.

X. *Composition and Discussion*

A. In Column I are the beginnings of sentences. In Column II are the completions to sentences of Column I. Select the completion best fitting each sentence in Column I according to the narrative. Read the completed sentences orally. Compose new sentences orally and discuss the narrative.

COLUMN I	COLUMN II
1. The students assemble	a. they just listen.
2. The students wait	b. but they are friendly.
3. Mr. Preston is	c. know each other by name.
4. Mr. Preston is delayed	d. many parts of the world.
5. There is a traffic jam.	e. to begin their lesson.
6. The teacher arrives	f. the language of the land.
7. The students are eager	g. five minutes later.
8. The students need to learn	h. on the freeway.
9. They come from	i. on his way to school.
10. The students don't	j. late for class.
11. Gail thinks Marcel	k. in the classroom.
12. The students are unable	l. for their teacher.
13. Marcel likes	m. cafeteria after the lesson.
14. The students eat in the	n. his American friends.
15. Some students don't talk ......,	o. to pronounce his name.
16. People have different customs ...	p. has a funny name.

B. 1. Tell us about your English class.
2. Tell us about your friends in class and at home.
3. Describe a classroom scene in your home town.
4. Tell about places on the map you are familiar with.

C. Read the poem aloud. Answer orally the questions listed following the poem.

Whispers of the Ages

*There are whispers[1]
In the mountains.
Do you hear them?*

[1] soft voice sounds

*There are whispers of
The ages,[2] telling
Tales,[3] can you hear?*

[2] times
[3] stories

There are whispers
Whispering tales
of many sages.[4]

[4] wise men

Can you hear?
Can you fathom[5]
All the wisdom[6] *of the ages?*

[5] understand
[6] learning,
    knowledge

1. Identify the *nouns* and *determiners* in this poem.
2. Identify the *verbs* in this poem.
3. Identify *declarative* sentences in simple present tense.
4. What is the title of this poem?
5. Which word recurs most frequently?
6. What is the *main idea* of this poem?
7. Do you like the poem? Don't you like it? Why?

D. Describe what you see in the picture below.

* * * * * *

Chapter Two

A Weekend in the County

Words to remember:

Present continuous tense

Adverbials of time:
*Saturday morning, every weekend,
minutes later, moments later, etc.*

Adverbials of frequency:
usually, sometimes, always, never, etc.

Words that describe (adjectives):
yellow, green, orange, black, etc.
good, modest, small, hilly, wet, trembling, happy, etc.

I.   *Narrative*

A.   The Campbells are a typical American family. Mr. Campbell is a lawyer. He works in Houston, Texas. He is a good lawyer. Mrs. Campbell is a housewife. She likes what she does; her husband, the attorney, likes his work too.

B.   The Campbells own an inexpensive cabin in La Grange, Texas. La Grange is a small town one hundred and five miles from Houston. The countryside is hilly, and the Colorado River runs through the town. The beauty of the countryside makes up for the discomfort of the living quarters.

C.   The Campbells are preparing for a weekend in their country home. Mrs. Campbell buys groceries at the supermarket. Tim and Ann help their mother. Tim is eight years old and a third grader. Ann is in junior high school. She is fourteen years old. Together the two children get up early Saturday morning. They are making sandwiches for the family. Mike and Lucy usually help their father with other chores. At the age of sixteen, Mike is the oldest child in the family. Lucy is the youngest in the family. She is only six years old.

D.   There are many rest areas on the highway. The Campbells sometimes stop to stretch. It's only a short distance to La Grange and they are eager to get there. There is a camping area near the river. People are always coming out to the river. There are boats and canoes for rent.

E.   "I'd like a canoe ride," Lucy says. Mike takes her for a canoe ride. "Sit still while I paddle," he tells her, "or else the canoe can overturn." "I always behave, don't I, Mike?" Lucy is smiling and Mike knows he cannot be cross with her.

F.   Twenty minutes later, the canoe is tossed by the rapids. Not far down the river are the falls. Mike wants to turn back, but the rapids carry the canoe toward the falls. Many canoes overturn there. He yells for help. Lucy is not a good swimmer. Mike is afraid she might drown.

G.   Soon, Mike loses control and the canoe tips over. "Hold on!" Mike yells at Lucy. But she cannot hear him. She is being dragged down toward the foaming falls. "My God! What can I do?" Mike thinks desperately. He feels helpless.

H.   Suddenly a state trooper appears near the falls. Without hesitation, the officer jumps into the water. Moments later, he is carrying little Lucy toward the place on shore where Mike is waiting.

I.   Dripping wet and trembling under the trooper's blanket, the two young Campbells are brought to the picnic grounds. "Thank you, officer!" Mrs. Campbell exclaims. "We worried so when they were late for supper," she adds with concern.

J.   "Not at all," the trooper responds. "Next time you must study the rapids before you get down that far." Everyone is happy now that Lucy and

Mike are safe. They are sitting by the fire warming themselves and toasting marshmallows. Lucy is smiling again.

* * *

II.   *Words in Context   [Pictographs]*

Below are the words used in the narrative. Where possible, each word has a [synonym], or it is defined as used in the story. Where possible, an (*antonym*) is also given. Make up sentences about the pictographs choosing the words you need. Read aloud.

Example: [lawyer] = Mr. Campbell is a lawyer in Houston.

A. and B.

Drawing of paragraphs A & B

typical **[usual]** (*unusual*); attorney **[lawyer]**; law **[rule]** (*disorder*); housewife **[married woman in charge of a household]** (*career woman*); occupation **[line of work]** (*leisure*); own **[possess]** (*lack*); inexpensive **[simple]** (*ostentatious*); cabin **[cottage]** (*mansion*); countryside **[rural area]** (*municipality*); hilly **[uneven terrain]** (*flat land*); run **[flow]** (*stand still*); make up **[compensate]** (*lack*); discomfort **[annoyance]** (*contentment*); living quarters **[residence]**

C. and D.

Drawing of paragraph C & D

groceries **[food]**; supermarket **[grocery store]**; chore **[task]** rest **[relax]** (*work*); area **[spot]**; stop **[halt]** (*go*); short **[small]** (*long*); distance **[remoteness]** (*closeness*); camping **[outing]**; near **[close]** (*distant*); weekend **[Saturday and Sunday]** (*weekday*); boat **[vessel]**; canoe **[rowboat]**; rent **[pay for the use of]**

E. and F.

Drawing of paragraph E & F

ride [**transport**]; be still [**at rest**] (*be active*); behave [**obey**] (*misbehave*); smile [**grin**] (*frown*); cross [**angry**] (*happy*); minute [**moment**]; toss [**fling**]; rapids [**rushing water**]; falls [**falling water**]; turn back [**turn around**] (*go ahead*); carry [**transport**]; toward [**in the direction of**] (*away from*); yell [**shout**] (*whisper*); swim [**stay afloat**] (*sink*); afraid [**frightened**] (*unafraid*); drown [**sink**] (*stay afloat*)

G. and H.

lose [**fail to keep**] (*gain*); control [**balance**]; tip over [**overturn**] (*stay upright*); hold on [**grip**] (*let go*); hear [**listen**] (*be deaf*); drag [**pull**]; foam [**froth**]; desperately [**hopelessly**] (*hopefully*); suddenly [**abruptly**] (*slowly*); appear [**become visible**] (*disappear*); hesitation [**pause**] (*haste*); officer [**official**]; dive [**plunge**]; shore [**bank**]

Drawing of paragraph G & H

I. and J.

wet [**moist**] (*dry*); tremble [**shake**] (*be still*); under [**beneath**] (*on top*); blanket [**covering**] ; young [**youthful**] (*old*); bring [**fetch**] (*send*); picnic [**outing**] ; exclaim [**cry out**] (*be silent*); worry [**concern**] (*unconcern*); late [**delayed**] (*early*); supper [**evening meal**] (*breakfast*); respond [**answer**] (*ignore*); before [**prior to**] (*after*); safe [**out of danger**] ; toast [**fry**]

III.   *Structures   [Phrases]*

Below are some phrases taken from the narrative. Make complete sentences and read them aloud.

A.	a	—	typical	—	family
B.	law	—	in	—	Houston

Drawings of paragraph I & J

C.	a	—	good	—	attorney
D.	likes	—	her occupation		
E.	a	—	modest	—	cabin
F.	a	—	small	—	town
G.	through	—	the	—	town
H.	of	—	the	—	living quarters
I.	for	—	a weekend		
J.	in	—	their	—	country house
K.	at	—	the	—	supermarket
L.	in	—	junior high		
M.	fourteen	—	years	—	old
N.	early	—	Saturday	—	morning
O.	for	—	the	—	family
P.	on	—	the	—	highway
Q.	a	—	short	—	distance
R.	out	—	to	—	the river
S.	for	—	a	—	canoe ride

T.	toward	—	the	—	falls
U.	near	—	the	—	falls
V.	into	—	the	—	water
W.	to	—	the	—	picnic grounds

IV. Sentences

A.   Read the following sentences aloud. Repeat, substituting, where possible, the synonym of the word in *italics,* or a phrase which explains the meaning. Make other necessary changes.

> Example: They own a *cabin.*
>   They own a *cottage.*

1. Mr. Campbell is an *attorney.*
2. Mrs. Campbell is a *housewife.*
3. She likes her *occupation.*
4. The countryside is *hilly.*
5. A river *runs* through the town.
6. They buy groceries at the *supermarket.*
7. There are many rest *areas* on the highway.
8. It's only a *short* distance.
9. The *rapids* carry them toward the falls.
10. Lucy is being *dragged* down the river.
11. He carries Lucy to the *shore.*
12. The Campbells are *concerned* about Lucy and Mike.

B.   Fill the blanks with words from the narrative. Each space may be filled by a word or phrase. Do not refer back to the narrative. Where possible, use variations of the missing words. Read aloud.

The Campbells are a _____ American _____ . Mr. Campbell is a _____.
He_____ as a lawyer. Mrs. Campbell is a _____ . She _____ what she does.
The Campbells_____ an _____cabin. The countryside in La Grange is
_____. The Colorado River_____ through _____ _____. This makes up
for the _____ of the _____quarters.
The Campbells are _____ for a _____ in their _____ home. Mrs.
Campbell buys _____ at the _____. Tim is eight_____old. Ann is in _____
school. They get up early_____ morning. They are _____sandwiches.
There are many_____ areas on the _____ . The Campbells stop to _____ .
It's only a _____ _____ to La Grange. They are_____to get there. The

camping area is _____ the _____ . There are _____ and _____ for _____ .

Mike takes _____ for a _____ ride. She sits _____ while he _____ . Mike can't be _____ at Lucy.

The canoe is _____ by the _____ . The falls are not _____ down the _____ . Mike wants to _____ back. The rapids _____ the _____ toward the _____ . Many canoes _____ there. Mike _____ for _____ . Lucy is not a _____ swimmer. Mike is _____ she might _____ .

Soon Mike _____ control. The canoe _____ _____ . "Hold _____ !" Mike _____ at Lucy. She cannot ___ ___ him. She is being _____ down toward the _____ falls. "What will I _____ mother and _____ ?" Mike thinks _____ .

Suddenly, a _____ trooper _____ near the _____ . Without _____ , the _____ dives into the _____ . Moments _____ , he is _____ Lucy _____ __ the place _____ .

_____ wet and _____ under the blanket, the two _____ Campbells are being _____ to the picnic _____ . "Thank you, _____ !" Mrs. Campbell _____ .

"Not at _____ ," the trooper _____ . Everyone is _____ now that Lucy and Mike are _____ . They are _____ at the fire _____ themselves and _____ . Lucy is _____ again.

V. Grammar and Syntax   (Points of Interest)

A.   The **Present Continuous Tense** expresses action in the PRESENT TIME. It is like the SIMPLE PRESENT TENSE, the NOW TENSE.

$$\text{Equation: } \begin{matrix} am \\ is \\ are \end{matrix} + verb + ing$$

PRESENT	PRESENT CONTINUOUS
He practices law.	He is practicing law.
They prepare for a weekend in the country.	They are preparing for a weekend in the country.
Mrs. Campbell buys groceries.	Mrs. Campbell is buying groceries.
Tim and Ann help their mother.	Tim and Ann are helping their mother.
They make sandwiches.	They are making sandwiches.
People come out to the river.	People are coming out to the river.

Mike thinks desperately.   Mike is thinking desperately.

They sit by the fire.   They are sitting by the fire.

_ _

B.   1. **Adverbials** of **time** answer the question **when?**

They get up early *Saturday morning.*
The Campbells go to La Grange *every weekend.*
Twenty *minutes later,* the canoe is tossed by the rapids.
Moments later, he is carrying Lucy to shore.

2. **Adverbials** of **frequency** answer the question **how often?**

Mike and Lucy *usually* help their father.
The Campbells *sometimes* stop to stretch.
People are *always* coming out to the river.
He knows that he can *never* be cross at Lucy.

_ _

C.   Words that describe (**Adjectives**) are:
1. Colors: yellow   green
            orange   black, etc.

or

2. Words such as:
   good   He is a *good* attorney.
   modest   They own a *modest* cabin.
   small   La Grange is a *small* town.
   hilly   The countryside is *hilly.*
   wet   She is *wet* and *trembling.*
   trembling
   happy   They are *happy* now.

VI.   *Word Recognition*

A.   Circle the word(s) in Column II most *like* the word in Column I, and the word(s) in Column III most *unlike* the word in Column I. This oral identification of words ought to be timed.

	COLUMN I		COLUMN II		COLUMN III
1.	**afraid**	a.	cross	a.	unafraid
		b.	frightened	b.	angry
		c.	pleased	c.	happy
2.	**behave**	a.	be at rest	a.	misbehave
		b.	smile	b.	be active
		c.	obey	c.	yell
3.	**buy**	a.	stop	a.	hinder
		b.	purchase	b.	work
		c.	rest	c.	sell
4.	**cabin**	a.	small house	a.	stream
		b.	river	b.	countryside
		c.	picnic	c.	mansion
5.	**desperately**	a.	hopelessly	a.	hopefully
		b.	suddenly	b.	slowly
		c.	abruptly	c.	hesitantly
6.	**discomfort**	a.	fear	a.	order
		b.	uneven terrain	b.	contentment
		c.	annoyance	c.	cabin
7.	**flow**	a.	practice	a.	stand still
		b.	yell	b.	lack
		c.	run	c.	go
8.	**hear**	a.	yell	a.	whisper
		b.	shout	b.	be deaf
		c.	listen	c.	sink
9.	**help**	a.	pass	a.	hinder
		b.	wait	b.	relax
		c.	assist	c.	hold on
10.	**hesitation**	a.	leisure	a.	hopelessness
		b.	pause	b.	desperation
		c.	fun	c.	haste
11.	**hilly**	a.	modest	a.	big
		b.	uneven terrain	b.	flat
		c.	distant	c.	small

12. **hold on**
    - a.   behave
    - b.   grip
    - c.   regulate
    - a.   let go
    - b.   tip over
    - c.   overturn

13. **late**
    - a.   under
    - b.   delayed
    - c.   below
    - a.   on top
    - b.   above
    - c.   early

14. **law**
    - a.   occupation
    - b.   rule
    - c.   chore
    - a.   practice
    - b.   career
    - c.   disorder

15. **lose**
    - a.   control
    - b.   regulate
    - c.   fail to keep
    - a.   tip over
    - b.   gain
    - c.   overturn

16. **modest**
    - a.   married
    - b.   usual
    - c.   inexpensive
    - a.   happy
    - b.   ostentatious
    - c.   nice

17. **occupation**
    - a.   line of work
    - b.   hobby
    - c.   boat
    - a.   work
    - b.   leisure
    - c.   smile

18. **own**
    - a.   stop
    - b.   possess
    - c.   help
    - a.   hinder
    - b.   sell
    - c.   lack

19. **rest**
    - a.   run
    - b.   relax
    - c.   ride
    - a.   sell
    - b.   work
    - c.   buy

20. **safe**
    - a.   warm
    - b.   hot
    - c.   protected
    - a.   unsafe
    - b.   cold
    - c.   far

21. **stop**
    - a.   halt
    - b.   swim
    - c.   drag
    - a.   buy
    - b.   wait
    - c.   go

22. **swim**
    - a.   carry
    - b.   stay afloat
    - c.   fall
    - a.   transport
    - b.   drive
    - c.   sink

23.	**typical**	a.	usual	a.	expensive
		b.	modest	b.	unusual
		c.	inexpensive	c.	simple

24.	**water**	a.	town	a.	hill
		b.	fluid	b.	froth
		c.	foam	c.	land

25.	**wet**	a.	moist	a.	dry
		b.	safe	b.	unsafe
		c.	well	c.	hilly

26.	**yell**	a.	drown	a.	whisper
		b.	shout	b.	stay afloat
		c.	toss	c.	be at rest

B. In the space on the left, write the word(s) that would best fit the expression in **bold print**. Make other necessary changes. Read aloud.

____ 1. The Campbells are a **usual** family.

____ 2. Mr. Campbell is an **attorney**.

____ 3. They **possess** a cabin in La Grange.

____ 4. The cabin is **simple**.

____ 5. They like visiting the **rural** area.

____ 6. The beauty **compensates** for the discomfort.

____ 7. They **purchase** groceries.

____ 8. The children prepare for the **outing**.

____ 9. They **assist** their Mother.

____ 10. The Campbells **relax** at the picnic.

____ 11. The **region** has a river.

____ 12. Mrs. Campbell buys groceries at the **supermarket**.

____ 13. There are **vessels** at the river.

____ 14. They **pay for the use of** a canoe.

____ 15. There are rest **spots** on the highway.

____ 16. The Campbells **halt** to stretch.

_____ 17. Mike cannot be **grumpy.**

_____ 18. He **grins** at Lucy.

_____ 19. **Moments** later there are the falls.

_____ 20. The rapids **transport** the boat.

_____ 21. They **yell** for help.

_____ 22. Mike is **afraid** Lucy might drown.

_____ 23. She tries **hopelessly** to keep afloat.

_____ 24. Mrs. Campbell worries when they are **delayed.**

_____ 25. They sit **protected** hear the fireplace.

VII.   Concept Recognition

Fill in the most appropriate word (phrase) to express the concept of the
sentence according to the narrative. Read the complete sentence aloud.

A.   The Campbells go to La Grange to _____ .

    1. relax   2. ride
    3. work   4. drive

B.   The beauty makes up for the _____ .

    1. ride   2. river
    3. discomfort   4. rest area

C.   The Campbells buy groceries to _____ .

    1. take home   2. prepare for the weekend.
    3. see the countryside   4. take on a boat ride

D.   Tim and Ann get up early Saturday to _____ .

    1. go to school   2. help their father
    3. drive to La Grange   4. make sandwiches

E.   The Campbells stop on the highway to _____ .

    1. stretch   2. study
    3. eat   4. read

F.   People are always coming out to the river because _____ .

   1. there are blankets   2. there are people
   3. there is a camping area   4. there is a trooper

G.   Mike tells Lucy to sit still because _____ .

   1. he likes her   2. the canoe can overturn
   3. she smiles   4. the family waits

H.   Lucy is smiling and Mike knows _____ .

   1. the boat will tip   2. Mother is waiting
   3. he swims well   4. he cannot be cross with her

I.   Mike yells for help because _____ .

   1. Lucy is not a good   2. he sees the trooper
      swimmer
   3. the falls are near   4. he sees his father

J.   Lucy cannot hear Mike because _____ .

   1. she swims away   2. she is being dragged
                                     down toward the falls
   3. she is on shore   4. the trooper is helping

K.   The trooper dives into the water to _____ .

   1. swim   2. help Lucy
   3. relax   4. help Mike

L.   The two young Campbells are trembling because _____ .

   1. they are dripping wet   2. they are at home
   3. they are under the   4. they are toasting marshmallows
      blanket

M.   Mrs. Campbell was worried _____ .

   1. when Lucy and Mike   2. when the trooper came
      return
   3. when Lucy and Mike   4. when Mr. Campbell yells
      were late for supper

N.   Before they go down far on the river _____ .

   1. they must rent a canoe   2. they must tell Mrs. Campbell

3. they must study the   4. they must tell no one
   rapids

O.   Everyone is happy because _____ .

1. Mrs. Campbell is worried 2. Lucy and Mike are safe
3. the trooper comes   4. the blanket is warm

P.   Lucy is smiling as she _____ .

1. sits by the fire   2. eats a sandwich
3. talks to Ann   4. swims in the rapids

VIII. Telling the Meaning

A.   Place a check mark (✓) in front of the word in Column II that best fits the
MEANING of the word in Column I. Read aloud a complete sentence
using this word.

COLUMN I   COLUMN II

1. **add**   _____ a.   subtract
                                _____ b.   respond
                                _____ c.   increase

2. **be still**   _____ a.   at rest
                                _____ b.   be active
                                _____ c.   be happy

3. **countryside**   _____ a.   municipality
                                _____ b.   cabin
                                _____ c.   rural area

4. **cross**   _____ a.   happy
                                _____ b.   angry
                                _____ c.   smile

5. **discomfort**   _____ a.   law
                                _____ b.   contentment
                                _____ c.   annoyance

6. **fail to keep**   _____ a.   lose
                                _____ b.   gain
                                _____ c.   hold on

7. **frightened**

_____ a. glad
_____ b. unafraid
_____ c. afraid

8. **ground**

_____ a. water
_____ b. earth
_____ c. picnic

9. **help**

_____ a. hinder
_____ b. assist
_____ c. flow

10. **hopelessly**

_____ a. suddenly
_____ b. desperately
_____ c. hopefully

11. **make up**

_____ a. lack
_____ b. sink
_____ c. compensate

12. **moist**

_____ a. dry
_____ b. wet
_____ c. young

13. **near**

_____ a. close
_____ b. distant
_____ c. short

14. **possess**

_____ a. want
_____ b. lose
_____ c. own

15. **profession**

_____ a. ·discomfort
_____ b. occupation
_____ c. leisure

16. **relax**

_____ a. rest
_____ b. work
_____ c. purchase

17. **short**

_____ a. hilly
_____ b. long
_____ c. small

18. **shout**
   - _____ a.   whisper
   - _____ b.   yell
   - _____ c.   drown

19. **simple**
   - _____ a.   ostentatious
   - _____ b.   inexpensive
   - _____ c.   typical

20. **small house**
   - _____ a.   mansion
   - _____ b.   cabin
   - _____ c.   river

21. **supper**
   - _____ a.   evening meal
   - _____ b.   picnic
   - _____ c.   breakfast

22. **turn back**
   - _____ a.   turn around
   - _____ b.   go on
   - _____ c.   carry

23. **uneven terrain**
   - _____ a.   hilly
   - _____ b.   flat land
   - _____ c.   stream

24. **usual**
   - _____ a.   unusual
   - _____ b.   typical
   - _____ c.   inexpensive

B.   Return to Exercise A. Place two check marks (✓✓) in front of the word in COLUMN II that is the ANTONYM of the word in COLUMN I. Read aloud a complete sentence using this word.

C.   Select one of the three (3) words (phrases) that best fulfills the MEANING of the sentence according to the narrative. Insert the word in the blank space. Read the completed sentence aloud.

1. The Campbells go to La Grange to take a _____ .
   a. rest   b. boat   c. canoe

2. They are not comfortable because the cabin is _____.
   a. hilly   b. small   c. typical

3. Mr. Campbell practices law. He is an _____ .
   a. housewife   b. attorney   c. trooper

4. A cabin is usually a small house in the _____ .
   a. municipality   b. countryside   c. residence

5. The countryside and the river _____ for the discomfort of the living quarters.
   a. compensate   b. lose   c. own

6. One of the chores in preparing for the picnic is _____ .
   a. renting a boat   b. buying groceries   c. relaxing

7. The Campbells stop on the highway to _____ .
   a. rent   b. assist   c. stretch

8. People are always coming out to the river because _____ .
   a. they buy groceries   b. they live in the   c. they rent boats and
                                    city   canoes

9. Lucy sits still. She's afraid the canoe can _____ .
   a. stop   b. stand   c. overturn

10. When Lucy smiles, Mike knows he cannot be _____ with her.
    a. cross   b. happy   c. still

11. Mike loses _____ and the canoe tips over.
    a. hold   b. control   c. Lucy

12. The rapids drag Lucy toward the falls. She cannot _____ Mike.
    a. hold on   b. lose   c. hear

13. The trooper dives into the river without _____ because Lucy is _____ .

    a. hesitation, drowning   b. haste, staying   c. a blanket, smiling afloat

14. Mrs. Campbell is worried when the young Campbells are _____ for the _____ .
    a. late, evening meal   b. absent, party   c. returned, river

15. The young Campbells tremble under the blanket because they are _____ .

    a. cold   b. crisp   c. soft

16. Now that the young Campbells are _____ everyone is _____ .
    a. far, unsafe   b. unsafe, warm   c. safe, happy

17. The fire is hot and they _____ marshmallows.
     a. increase　　　　　　b. toast　　　　　　c. rent

18. Lucy is smiling because she's _____ .
     a. safe　　　　　　b. hot　　　　　　c. near

IX. Comprehension　[Exercises]

A.　Place a check mark (✓) in front of the correct answer to each of the questions according to the narrative. Read the complete sentence aloud.

1. Who are the Campbells?

　　_____ a. They are friends.
　　_____ b. They are a typical American family.
　　_____ c. They are smiling.

2. Who practices law?

　　_____ a. Mr. Campbell.
　　_____ b. Mrs. Campbell.
　　_____ c. Mike.

3. Does Mrs. Campbell like being a housewife?

　　_____ a. Yes, she does.
　　_____ b. No, she doesn't.
　　_____ c. She thinks about it.

4. Why do the Campbells go to La Grange?

　　_____ a. They like to swim.
　　_____ b. They like their occupation.
　　_____ c. They own a small cabin.

5. How far is it to La Grange from Houston?

　　_____ a. Two hundred miles.
　　_____ b. One hundred and five miles.
　　_____ c. Twenty-five miles.

6. The Colorado River flows through

_____ a. the town.
_____ b. the highway.
_____ c. Houston.

7. What are Tim and Ann preparing?

_____ a. They help with the chores.
_____ b. They are making sandwiches.
_____ c. They are renting a canoe.

8. Who is the youngest in the family?

_____ a. Tim.
_____ b. Lucy.
_____ c. Mike.

9. Where are the rest areas?

_____ a. In Houston.
_____ b. On the river.
_____ c. On the highway.

10. When do the Campbells go to La Grange?

_____ a. Every day.
_____ b. On Saturday and Sunday.
_____ c. On Wednesday.

11. Why do people come out to the river?

_____ a. There are many people.
_____ b. There is water.
_____ c. There are boats and canoes.

12. Why must Lucy sit still?

_____ a. Because she is smiling.
_____ b. Because the canoe will overturn.
_____ c. Because Mike is afraid.

13. Why does Mike know he cannot be cross with Lucy?

_____ a. Because she is small.
_____ b. Because she is smiling.
_____ c. Because he is fifteen-years old.

14. How does the canoe tip over?

    ____ a. The trooper dives in.
    ____ b. Mike loses control.
    ____ c. Lucy is frightened.

15. Why does Mike yell for help?

    ____ a. Because Lucy is not a good swimmer.
    ____ b. Because he sees a trooper.
    ____ c. Because he is sad.

16. What does the trooper do?

    ____ a. He yells.
    ____ b. He dives into the water.
    ____ c. He smiles.

17. Why do the young Campbells tremble?

    ____ a. They are happy.
    ____ b. They are cold.
    ____ c. They are late.

18. What does the trooper say to the Campbells?

    ____ a. They must swim.
    ____ b. They must go to the cabin.
    ____ c. They must study the rapids.

19. Why is everyone happy?

    ____ a. Because they sit at the fire.
    ____ b. Because Lucy and Mike are safe.
    ____ c. Because they are toasting marshmallows.

B. Below are three (3) different thoughts expressed in each of the exercises. Assign the proper sequence (order) of **THOUGHT**, according to the narrative, by numbering 1 to 3. Read aloud.

1. a. in Houston, Texas   ____
   b. and he works   ____
   c. Mr. Campbell is a lawyer   ____

2. a. is a housewife and   ____
   b. Mrs. Campbell   ____
   c. she likes her occupation   ____

3. a. an inexpensive cabin in La Grange,   ————————
   b. Texas   ————————
   c. the Campbells own   ————————

4. a. the Colorado River   ————————
   b. the countryside is hilly, and   ————————
   c. flows through the town   ————————

5. a. one hundred and five   ————————
   b. La Grange is a small town   ————————
   c. miles from Houston   ————————

6. a. in their country home   ————————
   b. the Campbells are preparing   ————————
   c. for a weekend   ————————

7. a. at the supermarket   ————————
   b. buys groceries   ————————
   c. Mrs. Campbell   ————————

8. a. Saturday morning   ————————
   b. get up early   ————————
   c. together they   ————————

9. a. for the family   ————————
   b. making sandwiches   ————————
   c. they are   ————————

10. a. with other chores   ————————
    b. Mike and Lucy usually   ————————
    c. help their father   ————————

11. a. on the highway   ————————
    b. rest areas   ————————
    c. there are many   ————————

12. a. they are eager to get there   ————————
    b. it's only a short   ————————
    c. distance to La Grange and   ————————

13. a. coming out   ————————
    b. to the river   ————————
    c. people are always   ————————

14. a. boats and canoes
    b. for rent
    c. there are

15. a. be cross with her
    b. Lucy is smiling and
    c. Mike knows he cannot

16. a. tossed by the rapids
    b. the canoe is
    c. twenty minutes later,

17. a. the canoe toward the falls
    b. but the rapids carry
    c. Mike wants to turn back,

18. a. the canoe tips over
    b. Mike loses control and
    c. soon

19. a. toward the foaming falls
    b. dragged down
    c. she is

20. a. near the falls
    b. a state trooper appears
    c. suddenly,

21. a. into the water
    b. the officer dives
    c. without hesitation

22. a. he is carrying Lucy toward
    b. Mike is waiting
    c. the place on shore where

23. a. before you get down that far
    b. study the rapids
    c. next time you must

24. a. now that Lucy
    b. everyone is happy
    c. and Mike are safe

25. a. by the fire   _____
    b. toasting marshmallows   _____
    c. they are   _____

26. a. again   _____
    b. is smiling   _____
    c. Lucy   _____

C.   There are some statements listed below about the narrative. Write **T** for **True** in front of each statement that you think is true. Write **F** for **False** if the statement is not true. Read aloud.

_____ 1. The Campbells are a typical American family.

_____ 2. Mr. Campbell practices law.

_____ 3. Mrs. Campbell likes her occupation.

_____ 4. The Campbells own a mansion in La Grange.

_____ 5. The countryside is flat in La Grange.

_____ 6. Their cabin is comfortable.

_____ 7. The Campbells spend some weekends in La Grange.

_____ 8. They get up late on Saturday.

_____ 9. Mike and Lucy usually help their father.

_____ 10. Mike is the youngest in the family.

_____ 11. There are many rest areas on the highway.

_____ 12. It's a long distance to La Grange.

_____ 13. There is a camping area near the river.

_____ 14. People never come to the river.

_____ 15. There are boats for rent.

_____ 16. Mike tells Lucy to sit still.

_____ 17. The canoe is overturned by the rapids.

_____ 18. The rapids transport the canoe in the direction of the waterfalls.

_____ 19. Mike shouts for help.

_____ 20. Lucy stays afloat.

_____ 21. Mike fails to keep control of the canoe.

_____ 22. Lucy is being dragged up the river.

_____ 23. The state trooper dives into the water.

_____ 24. Mrs. Campbell is thankful.

_____ 25. The young Campbells sit near the fire.

_____ 26. Everyone is happy now that they are safe.

X.   *Composition and Discussion*

A.   In Column I are beginnings of sentences. In Column II are the completions
to the sentences of Column I. Select the completion best fitting each
sentence in Column I according to the narrative. Read the completed
sentences orally. Compose new sentences orally and discuss the narrative.

COLUMN I	COLUMN II
1. The Campbells are	a. is a housewife.
2. Mrs. Campbell	b. a typical American family.
3. The Campbells	c. are safe.
4. The countryside	d. flows through the town.
5. The Colorado River	e. before you get down that far.
6. The Campbells are preparing	f. to the camping ground.
7. They are making	g. "Thank you, officer!"
8. There are many	h. smiling again.
9. There is a camping area	i. and toasting marshmallows.
10. People are always	j. own an inexpensive cabin.
11. Mike takes Lucy	k. for a weekend in their country home.
12. The trooper brings Lucy	l. sandwiches for the family.
13. Lucy and Mike are brought	m. rest areas on the highway.
14. Mrs. Campbell exclaims	n. near the river.
15. You must study the rapids	o. for a canoe ride.
16. Mike and Lucy	p. safely to shore.
17. They are sitting by the fire	q. coming out to the river.
18. Lucy is	r. is hilly.

B.   1. Tell us about your family.
2. Describe a river you know.
3. Describe the countryside where you live.
4. Tell us about an outing you have gone on.
5. Tell us about your home.

C.   Describe what you see in the picture below.

D.   Read the poem aloud. Answer orally the questions listed following the poem.

Hope

The hope for better times to come
is stronger than the will
to end the pain[1]   [1] hurt
at once. . .

In quiet meditation[2] *I spend*   [2] contemplation,
my free moments. In   thought
bitterness[3] *end*   [3] sadness
my thoughts.

Nothing remains but hope
that better times
must come,

if only the will[4] to   [4] desire
live is strong
enough. . .

    1. Identify the *adjectives* in this poem.
    2. Identify the *main idea.*
    3. What is the meaning of the third stanza?
    4. Which stanza expresses optimism?
    5. What idea is expressed in the last stanza?

* * * * * *

Chapter Three

The
Philanthropist

```
Words to remember:

Simple past tense
Past continuous

Indefinite pronouns:
every-      -body
any-        -one
some-       -thing
no-

Question words:
what? where? who?
when? why? how?


Adjective              Comparative              Superlative
  old                    older                    oldest
```

I. Narrative

A.   Curtis Smith came from a Negro family of nine. At the age of sixteen, he was the second oldest child in the family. He came from the "wrong side of the tracks," as the saying goes. The house where he lived was overcrowded, but clean. Mrs. Smith was an able housekeeper. She managed on very little income.

B.   Now Curtis was in trouble. Mr. and Mrs. Smith called on Mr. Campbell to seek counsel. Curtis was a friend of Mike Campbell. He attended Mike's high school when the busing was ordered. The authorities intended to offer equal educational opportunity to children of lower income households. This brought Mike and Curtis together. Both were on the varsity football team. They became friends quickly.

C.   Mr. Campbell listened attentively. He made many notes which he intended to use in court. He assured Mr. and Mrs. Smith that he was going to do all he could for Curtis. "Don't you worry, it isn't as bad as it seems." "The police were kind," Mrs. Smith said. "They allowed Curtis to call me." "That wasn't kindness, Mrs. Smith. The one phone call was his constitutional right," Mr. Campbell assured her.

D.   The warehouse guards pointed accusing fingers at Curtis. They testified that he was the man who broke into the warehouse. Those present in the courtroom whispered: "Somebody ought to do something about it!" "First they take over our schools, then they steal from us." "What's next?" "They should stay where they belong!" The judge rapped his gavel. Curits' friends and neighbors maintained his innocence. They declared under oath that he was a good boy who never did wrong.

E.   The judge was confused. The court must know beyond a reasonable doubt that a man is guilty. He cannot be convicted otherwise. The judge thought of a plan whereby everyone could benefit. A thorough investigation of Curtis' personal activities was ordered. The court recessed for one week.

F.   When the court reconvened, the following was revealed by the investigation: When Curtis first came to Euclid High, his peers avoided him. Even when he was accepted as a tackle on the team, they did not treat him as an equal. They came from well-to-do families. He did not belong.

G.   When the war broke out overseas, the team adopted an orphanage in a small town. Each month a contribution was sent there which helped to sustain the war victims. Curtis wanted to contribute. He began by breaking into small stores. The money which he received for the stolen goods went to the orphanage. He became one of the team.

H.   "This was the reason why Curtis stole, your Honor," Mr. Campbell ended his plea. "We throw ourselves on the mercy of the court." The judge deliberated quietly with the prosecuting attorney. Moments later, the judge spoke.

I. "In view of the circumstances, we cannot take stern measures against the accused, Curtis Smith. We pass a suspended sentence, and place Curtis Smith in the custody of his parents."

* * *

II. Words in Context   [Pictographs]

Below are some of the words used in the narrative. Where possible, each word has a [synonym]; or it is defined as used in the story. Where possible, an (*antonym*) is also given. Make up sentences about the pictographs choosing the words you need. Read aloud.

Example: [philanthropist] = This story tells about a philanthropist.

A. and B.

Drawing of paragraph A & B

philanthropist [**humanitarian**] (*misanthrope*); wrong side of tracks [**ill-bred**] (*well-bred*); overcrowded [**congested**] (*spacious*); clean [**sanitary**] (*dirty*); able [**competent**] (*unable*); least [**minimum**] (*most*); deep [**profound**] (*shallow*); trouble [**distress**] (*tranquility*); call on [**visit**] (*leave*); seek [**look for**] (*find*); counsel [**advise**] ; attend [**be present**] (*be absent*); busing* [**transporting**] ; order [**command**] ; authority [**power**] ; offer [**give**] (*rescind*); equal [**same**] (*unequal*); low [**small**] (*high*); income [**salary**] ; together [**jointly**] (*separately*); team [**group**] (*individual*); quickly [**rapidly**] (*slowly*)

C. and D.

Drawing of paragraph C & D

listen [**hear**] (*ignore*); attentively [**closely**] (*negligently*); court [**tribunal**] ; assure [**pledge**] ; worse [**more unfavorable**] (*better*); kind [**sympathetic**]

---

*In order to integrate schools, authorities ordered that students from one section of a town be transported to another. This was called "busing."

(*unkind*); allow [permit] (*deny*); constitutional [inherent]; right [prerogative]; warehouse [storage building]; guard [sentry]; point at [single out]; accusing [incriminating]; break into [make illegal entry]; testify [witness]; somebody [someone] (*nobody*); something [anything] (*nothing*); take over [dominate] (*give up*); innocence [lack of guilt] (*guilt*); declare [affirm] (*stifle*); wrong [error] (*right*)

E. and F.

Drawing of paragraph E & F

confused [perplexed] (*orderly*); beyond [past] (*near*); reasonable [rational] (*unreasonable*); doubt [uncertainty] (*certainty*); guilty [at fault] (*innocent*); convicted [found guilty] (*acquitted*); benefit [profit] (*lose*); thorough [complete] (*careless*); investigation [examination]; personal [private] (*public*); activity [action] (*inactivity*); recess [pause] (*reconvene*); reconvene [meet again] (*recess*); follow [succeed] (*precede*); reveal [disclose] (*cover up*); first [original] (*last*); peer [equal] (*unequal*); avoid [shun] (*accept*); consent [approve] (*reject*); well-to-do [rich] (*poor*)

G. and H. and I.

Drawing of paragraph G, H & I

war [**conflict**] (*peace*); break out [**begin**] (*end*); adopt [**support**] (*discard*); orphanage [**institution for children without parents**] ; contribute [**donate**] (*receive*); victim [**prey**] (*aggressor*); sustain [**support**] (*release*); steal [**rob**] (*buy*); plea [**request**] ; mercy [**pity**] (*severity*); deliberate [**consider**] ; quietly [**silently**] (*noisily*); chance [**happenstance**] (*planned action*); stern [**severe**] (*lenient*); against [**opposed**] (*for*); suspend [**dismiss**] ; sentence [**judgment**] (*acquittal*); place in custody [**legal guardianship**]

III. Structures (Phrases)

Below are some *phrases* taken from the narrative. Make complete sentences and read them aloud.

A.	from	—	a	—	Negro family
B.	at	—	the	—	age
C.	the	—	second	—	oldest
D.	in	—	the	—	family
E.	from	—	the	—	other side
F.	where	—	he	—	lived
G.	an	—	able	—	housekeeper
H.	with	—	the	—	least
I.	in	—	deep	—	trouble
J.	to	—	seek	—	counsel
K.	of	—	Mike Campbell		
L.	when	—	the	—	busing
M.	to	—	offer	—	educational
N.	of	—	lower	—	income
O.	on	—	the	—	varsity
P.	to	—	use	—	in court
Q.	to	—	do	—	all he could
R.	the	—	one	—	phone call
S.	who	—	broke	—	into
T.	where	—	they	—	belong
U.	who	—	never	—	did
V.	that	—	a man	—	is guilty
W.	for	—	one	—	week
X.	him	—	as	—	an equal
Y.	into	—	small	—	stores
Z.	at	—	the	—	mercy

IV. Sentences

A. Read the following sentences aloud. Repeat, substituting where possible, the synonym of the word in *italics*, or a phrase that explains the meaning. Make other necessary changes.

1. The house was *overcrowded*.
2. Mrs. Smith was an *able* housekeeper.
3. Curtis was in deep *trouble*.
4. The *busing* was ordered.
5. They *offered* equal opportunity.
6. Mr. Campbell listened *attentively*.
7. They *allowed* Curtis to call.
8. It was his *constitutional* right.

9. The *guards* accused Curtis.
10. They maintained his *innocence.*
11. The judge was *confused.*
12. A thorough *investigation* was ordered.
13. The court *reconvened.*
14. They did not treat him as an *equal.*
15. The team adopted an *orphanage.*
16. Curtis wanted to *contribute.*
17. The judge was not *stern.*
18. Curtis was placed in the *custody* of his parents.

B.   Fill in the blanks with words from the narrative. Each space may be filled by a word or phrase. Do not refer back to the narrative. Where possible, use variations of the missing words. Read aloud.

Curtis_____ from a Negro_____. He_____ the second_____child. The house_____ he lived _____ overcrowded. Mrs. Smith _____ on very _____income.

Curtis _____ in deep _____. He was a _____ of Mike. He _____ Mike's school. The busing _____ ordered.

The authorities_____ to offer equal _____. Mike and Curtis _____ on the varsity football _____. They_____ friends.

Mr. Campbell_____ attentively. He _____ many notes. He was going to _____ them in _____. They_____Curtis to _____. It was his_____ right.

The guards _____ accusing _____. They _____that Curtis _____ into the warehouse. The judge_____ his gavel. The neighbors_____his innocence. They_____ he was a_____boy.

The judge was_____. A man must be_____ beyond_____ doubt. He can _____be convicted _____. The _____ of a plan. A_____ investigation was_____.

The_____ revealed the_____. At first his _____avoided Curtis. They did not _____ him as an _____. They came from _____ families. He _____ not_____.

The team_____ an orphanage. A _____ was sent each _____. Curtis _____ to contribute. He_____ into small_____. He gave the _____ to the orphanage. He was one_____ team.

Mr. Campbell _____ his plea. The judge _____ silently. _____ later the _____spoke. "We_____ a suspended _____." Curtis was _____ in the custody of his _____.

V. *Grammar and Syntax* *(Points of Interest)*

A. **Simple Past Tense.** Regular verbs form their past tense by adding *-ed* or *-d* to the verb.

Example: attend*ed*   visit*ed*   call*ed*
           listen*ed*   assur*ed*   accus*ed*

Curtis *attended* Euclid High.
She *visited* Mr. Campbell.
She *called* on Mr. Campbell.
The authorities *intended* to offer equal education.
They *allowed* Curtis to call.

PAST TENSE is used to:

1. State facts about past conditions or events.
      The team *adopted* an orphanage.
      Mr. Campbell *assured* her.
      His neighbors *testified.*

2. Make general statements about a particular time.
      When the court *reconvened*, the following was revealed.
      Last year he was *accepted* as a tackle.
      Every month they *contributed* to the orphanage.

Some verbs have an irregular* pattern of the PAST TENSE.

PRESENT		PAST		
be	—	was	—	were
go	—	went		
do	—	did		
break	—	broke		
can	—	could		

Can is a modal auxiliary.

Examples of past tense:

He *was* the second oldest.
Curtis never *did* wrong.
The war *broke out* overseas.

— — — — — — — — — — — — — — — — — —

B. **Past Continuous.** The continuous form of the past tense expresses action still happening.

Equation: $\left.\begin{array}{c} was \\ were \end{array}\right\}$ + verb + *-ing*

PAST	PAST CONTINUOUS
The war *broke out*.	The war *was breaking out*.
He *broke into* the store.	He was *breaking* into a store.
They *contributed* to an orphanage.	They *were contributing* to an orphanage.

— — — — — — — — — — — — — — — — — —

C.   1. **Indefinite Pronouns** refer to *unknown persons* or *things*, or to *indefinite quantities.* The indefinite pronouns are the words in COLUMN I plus the words in COLUMN II.

I		II
every		*-body*
any-	+	*-one*
some-		*-thing*
no-		

Result:

everybody	*everyone*	*everything*
anybody	*anyone*	*anything*
somebody	*someone*	*something*
nobody	*no one*	*nothing*

2. The form of the verb we use with the indefinite pronoun is the same form as would be used with the pronoun *he*.*

Note: The verb form is that of the pronoun *he* (singular) because these words end in *-body, -one*, and *-thing.*

Somebody has to do something.
Everyone points his finger at Curtis.
Everybody enjoys football.

— — — — — — — — — — — — — — — — — — —

D. **Question words** are:

1. *What* . . . . .was ordered?

2. *Where** . . . . .are the people?

3. *Who* . . . . .is accused of stealing?

4. *When* . . . . .do they go to court?

5. *Why*** . . . . .are they accusing Curtis?

6. *How* . . . . .can they say this?

— — — — — — — — — — — — — — — — — — —

E. Words that **Describe** or **Qualify** come in three (3) degrees:

1. Adjective   A *good* friend is hard to find.
2. Comparative   He is a *better* student than I.
3. Superlative   Curtis was the second *oldest* child in the family.

To compare regular adjectives of one syllable we add *-er, -est*. Adjectives of more than one syllable use the words *more* and *most*.

1. Adjective   He is an *old* friend.
2. Comparative   Mike is an *older* child than Ann.
3. Superlative   He was the *oldest* child in the family.

— — — — — — — — — — — — — — — — — — —

F. **Adjective [Relative] Clauses.** The adjective clause generally modifies a preceding noun or a pronoun.

*Where needs the response *in, on,* or *at.* (*Where* is he? He's *in* court.)

**Why often needs the response *because.* (*Why* do the guards say that? *Because* they saw Curtis in the warehouse.)

a time	*when*	He attended Mike's high school *when* busing was ordered.
a place	*where*	The house *where* he lived was clean.
a reason	*why*	This was the reason *why* Curtis stole.
a person	*who, whom* or *whose* or *that*	They declared *that* he was a good boy *who* never did wrong.
a thing	*which* or *that*	The court must know *that* a man is guilty.

Note: The relative word *where* is sometimes used without denoting place. (The judge thought of a plan *whereby* everyone could profit most.)

VI. *Word Recognition*

A.   Circle the word(s) in Column II most *like* the word in Column I, and the word(s) in Column III most *unlike* the word in Column I. This oral identification of words ought to be timed.

COLUMN I		COLUMN II		COLUMN III
1. **able**	a.	adequate	a.	least
	b.	spacious	b.	unable
	c.	clean	c.	inexpensive
2. **accept**	a.	equal	a.	reject
	b.	see	b.	look
	c.	approve	c.	meet
3. **against**	a.	competent	a.	lenient
	b.	opposed	b.	for
	c.	with someone	c.	considerate
4. **allow**	a.	point at	a.	deny
	b.	permit	b.	single out
	c.	incriminate	c.	accuse
5. **attend**	a.	call	a.	dispatch
	b.	be present	b.	deter
	c.	advise	c.	be absent

6. **benefit**	a.	profit	a.	care
	b.	work	b.	lose
	c.	complete	c.	earn

7. **call on**	a.	seek	a.	dispatch
	b.	look for	b.	find
	c.	visit	c.	leave

8. **confused**	a.	perplexed	a.	near
	b.	glad	b.	far
	c.	happy	c.	orderly

9. **declare**	a.	ask	a.	work
	b.	affirm	b.	stifle
	c.	seek	c.	answer

10. **deep**	a.	spacious	a.	congested
	b.	profound	b.	shallow
	c.	least	c.	most

11. **doubt**	a.	guilt	a.	certainty
	b.	uncertainty	b.	innocence
	c.	fault	c.	acquittal

12. **follow**	a.	succeed	a.	cover up
	b.	cooperate	b.	avoid
	c.	disclose	c.	precede

13. **listen**	a.	believe	a.	ignore
	b.	hear	b.	answer
	c.	say	c.	assure

14. **parents**	a.	custody	a.	children
	b.	mother and father	b.	orphanage
	c.	legal guardianship	c.	judge

15. **philanthropist**	a.	well-bred person	a.	misanthrope
	b.	clean person	b.	lower class person
	c.	humanitarian	c.	dirty person

16. **quietly**	a.	silently	a.	severely
	b.	leniently	b.	sternly
	c.	suspended	c.	noisily

17.	**sentence**	a.	judgment	a.	condemnation
		b.	suspension	b.	story
		c.	trust	c.	dismissal
18.	**somebody**	a.	something	a.	nobody
		b.	sentry	b.	anything
		c.	someone	c.	nothing
19.	**take over**	a.	break into	a.	give up
		b.	dominate	b.	be innocent
		c.	illegal entry	c.	lack guilt
20.	**together**	a.	without	a.	separately
		b.	anyhow	b.	individually
		c.	jointly	c.	quickly
21.	**trouble**	a.	busing	a.	tranquility
		b.	transporting	b.	counsel
		c.	distress	c.	advise
22.	**victim**	a.	mercy	a.	aggressor
		b.	pity	b.	severity
		c.	prey	c.	deliberation
23.	**war**	a.	break out	a.	peace
		b.	conflict	b.	end
		c.	begin	c.	support
24.	**worse**	a.	more unfavorable	a.	sympathetic
		b.	unkind	b.	better
		c.	oldest	c.	kind

B. In the space on the left write the word(s) that best fit the expression in **bold print**. Make other necessary changes. Read aloud.

_____ 1. Curtis Smith was a **humanitarian**.

_____ 2. He was sixteen years **of age**.

_____ 3. Curtis came from the **lower class**.

_____ 4. The Smith house was **not spacious**.

_____ 5. But it **wasn't dirty**.

_____ 6. Mrs. Smith was an **adequate** housekeeper.

_____ 7. Curtis was in **profound** trouble.

_____ 8. Mr. Campbell gave his **advice**.

_____ 9. The authorities **commanded** busing.

_____ 10. They **gave** him equal education.

_____ 11. Mr. Campbell received a good **salary**.

_____ 12. Curtis was a member of a **group**.

_____ 13. He became Mike's friend **rapidly**.

_____ 14. The judge **heard** the witnesses.

_____ 15. He listened **closely**.

_____ 16. The court **pledged** justice.

_____ 17. The witnesses were **sympathetic**.

_____ 18. The court **permitted** a small recess.

_____ 19. This was Curtis' **inherent** right.

_____ 20. The neighbors **affirmed** his innocence.

_____ 21. Everyone was **perplexed**.

_____ 22. Everybody would **benefit**.

_____ 23. The court **met again** on the next day.

_____ 24. They heard Mr. Campbell's **request**.

_____ 25. The judge was **not severe**.

VII.   *Concept Recognition*

Fill in the most appropriate word (phrase) to express the CONCEPT of the sentence according to the narrative. Read the complete sentence aloud.

A.   Mrs. Smith came to Mr. Campbell to seek _____ .

   1. counsel   2. Mike
   3. Curtis   4. her household

B.   Curtis came from the _____ side of the tracks.

   1. good   2. dirty
   3. wrong   4. clean

C. Curtis attended Mike's high school because the busing was_____ .

  1. summoned   2. ordered
  3. dispatched   4. trouble

D. The busing was commanded in order to offer_____ educational opportunity.

  1. deep   2. least
  3. profound   4. equal

E. Mike and Curtis were friends because they were on the same_____.

  1. authority   2. expense
  3. team   4. salary

F. The police allowed Curtis to call because it was_____.

  1. kindness   2. his constitutional right
  3. advice   4. his mother

G. Curtis was before the court because he was____ ___ of breaking into a __ ___ .

  1. permitted, school   2. tired, court
  3. accused, warehouse   4. proud, tribunal

H. The court was confused because Curtis' neighbors_____that he was a good boy.

  1. declared   2. take over
  3. repressed   4. break into

I. The judge ordered an investigation whereby everyone would_____ .

  1. benefit   2. recess
  3. lose   4. reveal

J. The investigation was to _____ the truth.

  1. cover up   2. reveal
  3. precede   4. follow

K. Curtis stole in order to _____ the money to the orphanage.

  1. contribute   2. plead
  3. receive   4. dismiss

VIII. *Telling the Meaning*

A. Place a check mark (✓) in front of the word in COLUMN II that best fits the MEANING of the word in COLUMN I. Read aloud a complete sentence using this word.

COLUMN I   COLUMN II

1. **affirm**
    _____ a.   right
    _____ b.   stifle
    _____ c.   declare

2. **assure**
    _____ a.   pledge
    _____ b.   better
    _____ c.   deny

3. **be present**
    _____ a.   attend
    _____ b.   be absent
    _____ c.   defer

4. **beyond**
    _____ a.   farther
    _____ b.   near
    _____ c.   most

5. **contribute**
    _____ a.   donate
    _____ b.   receive
    _____ c.   prey

6. **distress**
    _____ a.   counsel
    _____ b.   tranquility
    _____ c.   trouble

7. **income**
    _____ a.   expense
    _____ b.   salary
    _____ c.   wealth

8. **judgment**
    _____ a.   dismissal
    _____ b.   sentence
    _____ c.   custody

9. **listen**
    _____ a.   hear
    _____ b.   ignore
    _____ c.   look

10. **low**
_____ a. high
_____ b. small
_____ c. near

11. **mother and father**
_____ a. parents
_____ b. children
_____ c. legal guardianship

12. **offer**
_____ a. give
_____ b. rescind
_____ c. equal

13. **overcrowded**
_____ a. congested
_____ b. spacious
_____ c. clean

14. **peer**
_____ a. equal
_____ b. unequal
_____ c. well-to-do

15. **permit**
_____ a. do
_____ b. deny
_____ c. allow

16. **perplexed**
_____ a. confused
_____ b. orderly
_____ c. able

17. **personal**
_____ a. public
_____ b. private
_____ c. known

18. **profound**
_____ a. shallow
_____ b. deep
_____ c. least

19. **reconvene**
_____ a. pause
_____ b. recess
_____ c. meet again

20. **reveal**
_____ a. disclose
_____ b. cover up
_____ c. precede

21. **someone**   _____ a.   somebody
                                 _____ b.   nobody
                                 _____ c.   something

22. **steal**   _____ a.   buy
                                 _____ b.   rob
                                 _____ c.   break out

23. **unable**   _____ a.   able
                                 _____ b.   least
                                 _____ c.   incompetent

24. **visit**   _____ a.   call on
                                 _____ b.   dispatch
                                 _____ c.   depart

B.   Return to Exercise A. Place two check marks (√√) in front of the word in COLUMN II that is the ANTONYM of the word in COLUMN I. Read aloud a complete sentence using this word.

C.   Select one of the three (3) words (phrases) that best fulfills the MEANING of the sentence according to the narrative. Insert the word in the blank space. Read the completed sentence aloud.

1. Curtis Smith was in trouble because he wanted to be a _____.
   a. misanthrope   b. philanthropist   c. teacher

2. Mrs. Smith managed on very little income because she was _____.
   a. an able housekeeper   b. Curtis' mother   c. overcrowded

3. The busing was ordered to offer children equal _____.
   a. education   b. law   c. income

4. Mr. Campbell was a good _____ and he _____ attentively.
   a. man, looked   b. friend, talked   c. lawyer, listened

5. Curtis was _____ one call because it was his _____.
   a. given, custody call   b. allowed,   c. ordered, mother
                                    constitutional right   talking

6. To convict a man the court must know beyond a reasonable
   that a man is _____.
   a. doubt, guilty   b. thought, covered up   c. doubt, innocent

7. The judge _____ an _____ of Curtis' personal activities.
   a. dispersed, court   b. ordered,   c. covered up,
                                 investigation   examination

8. The court _____ to _____ time for the examination.
   a. reconvened, convict   b. met again,   c. recessed, allow
                                   disperse

9. Curtis' peers avoided him at first because he was _____.
   a. not well-to-do   b. a tackle   c. a bad boy

10. The money was donated to the orphanage to _____ the war orphans.
    a. consider   b. discard   c. sustain

11. The judge was _____ because Curtis stole to _____ to the orphanage.
    a. lenient, contribute   b. severe, give   c. deliberate, travel

IX. *Comprehension* *[Exercises]*

A.   Place a check mark (✓) in front of the correct response to each of the statements according to the narrative. Read the complete sentence aloud.

1. At the age of sixteen, Curtis was

    _____ a. the oldest of the children.
    _____ b. the second oldest of the children.
    _____ c. the best of the children.

2. The house where Curtis lived

    _____ a. was overcrowded.
    _____ b. was wrong.
    _____ c. was old.

3. Mrs. Smith was an able housekeeper because

    _____ a. she came to Mr. Campbell.
    _____ b. she knew Mike.
    _____ c. she managed on very little income.

4. Mrs. Smith came to Mr. Campbell because

    _____ a. she was a good housekeeper.

_____ b. she was his friend.
_____ c. Curtis was in deep trouble.

5. Curtis was Mike's friend. They were on the

_____ a. football team together.
_____ b. wrong side of the tracks.
_____ c. orphanage.

6. The busing was intended for

_____ a. the Campbell family.
_____ b. the children of lower income households.
_____ c. the law.

7. Mr. Campbell took notes to use them

_____ a. in court.
_____ b. at home.
_____ c. for Mike.

8. Mr. Campbell assured Mrs. Smith

_____ a. that Curtis was innocent.
_____ b. that he would do all he could.
_____ c. that the police were kind.

9. The one phone call at the police station

_____ a. is a constitutional right.
_____ b. is a police kindness.
_____ c. is not a right of everyone.

10. The people whispered in the courtroom

_____ a. because they were kind.
_____ b. because they were unkind.
_____ c. because they liked Curtis.

11. The judge rapped his gavel

_____ a. for the recess.
_____ b. to restore silence.
_____ c. to maintain Curtis' innocence.

12. The judge ordered an investigation

_____ a. of Curtis' friends.

_____ b. of Curtis' personal activities.
_____ c. of the guards.

13. Curtis gave the money

　_____ a. to his friends.
　_____ b. to the football team.
　_____ c. to the orphanage.

14. When Curtis contributed, he became

　_____ a. a victim
　_____ b. a tackle.
　_____ c. one of the team.

15. The judge was kind because he

　_____ a. gave a suspended sentence.
　_____ b. rapped his gavel.
　_____ c. deliberated quietly.

B. Below there are three (3) different thoughts expressed in each of the exercises. Assign the proper sequence (order) of THOUGHT, according to the narrative, by numbering 1 to 3. Read aloud.

1. a. he was the second oldest _____
   b. at the age of sixteen _____
   c. child in the family _____

2. a. where he lived _____
   b. was overcrowded but clean _____
   c. the house _____

3. a. called on Mr. Campbell _____
   b. to seek counsel _____
   c. Mrs. Smith _____

4. a. of lower income households _____
   b. the authorities intended to offer _____
   c. equal educational opportunity to children _____

5. a. to use in court _____
   b. he made many notes _____
   c. which he was going _____

6. a. to do all he could for Curtis   _____
    b. that he was going   _____
    c. he assured Mrs. Smith   _____

7. a. constitutional right   _____
    b. was his   _____
    c. the one phone call   _____

8. a. fingers at Curtis   _____
    b. the warehouse guards   _____
    c. pointed accusing   _____

9. a. they testified   _____
    b. broke into the warehouse   _____
    c. he was the man who   _____

10. a. and then they steal from us   _____
    b. over our schools   _____
    c. first they take   _____

11. a. they belong   _____
    b. stay where   _____
    c. they should   _____

12. a. his innocence   _____
    b. Curtis' friends and   _____
    c. neighbors maintained   _____

13. a. who never did wrong   _____
    b. that he was a good boy   _____
    c. they declared under oath   _____

14. a. doubt that a man is guilty   _____
    b. must know beyond reasonable   _____
    c. the court   _____

15. a. activities was ordered   _____
    b. of Curtis' personal   _____
    c. a thorough investigation   _____

16. a. by the investigation   _____
    b. the following was revealed   _____
    c. when the court reconvened   _____

17. a. they did not treat him as an equal   _____
    b. even when he was accepted   _____
    c. as a tackle on the team   _____

18. a. an orphanage in a small town   _____
    b. the team adopted   _____
    c. when the war broke out overseas   _____

19. a. to sustain the war victims   _____
    b. was sent there which helped   _____
    c. each month a contribution   _____

20. a. for the stolen goods   _____
    b. went to the orphanage   _____
    c. the money which he received   _____

21. a. quietly with   _____
    b. the prosecuting attorney   _____
    c. the judge deliberated   _____

22. a. we cannot take stern   _____
    b. in view of the circumstances   _____
    c. measures against the accused   _____

23. a. in the custody   _____
    b. of his parents   _____
    c. we place Curtis Smith   _____

C. There are some statements listed below about the narrative. Write **T** for **True** in front of each statement that you think is true. Write **F** for **False** if the statement is not true. Read aloud.

_____ 1. Curtis Smith was a Negro.

_____ 2. He was the second oldest in his family.

_____ 3. The house where Curtis lived was spacious.

_____ 4. The Smith family was well-to-do.

_____ 5. Curtis was in no trouble.

_____ 6. Curtis was Mike Campbell's friend.

_____ 7. The busing was ordered by the authorities.

_____ 8. Mike and Curtis were on the football team.

____ 9. Mr. Campbell did not listen to Mrs. Smith.

____ 10. He promised to do all he could for Curtis.

____ 11. The judge was perplexed.

____ 12. He ordered a complete examination.

____ 13. Those present in the courtroom whispered.

____ 14. Curtis' neighbors pointed accusing fingers.

____ 15. He could be convicted on reasonable doubt.

____ 16. When Curtis came to Euclid High his peers liked him.

____ 17. They treated him like an equal.

____ 18. Curtis did not want to contribute to the orphanage.

____ 19. He took money from the war victims.

____ 20. The judge deliberated noisily with the prosecuting attorney.

____ 21. The court took stern measures with Curtis.

X. *Composition and Discussion*

A. In COLUMN I are the beginnings of sentences. In COLUMN II are the completions to sentences of COLUMN I. Select the completion best fitting each sentence in COLUMN I according to the narrative. Read the completed sentences orally. Compose new sentences orally and discuss the narrative.

COLUMN I

1. Curtis Smith came . . . .
2. At the age of sixteen . . . .
3. The home where Curtis lived . . .
4. Mrs. Smith managed . . . .
5. Curtis Smith attended . . . . . .
6. The busing was ordered . . . . . .
7. Mike and Curtis were . . . .
8. Mr. Campbell made . . . .
9. He was going to do all . . . .
10. The phone call was . . . .

COLUMN II

a. in the custody of his parents.
b. lenient with Curtis.
c. he was the second oldest.
d. by the authorities.
e. on very little income.
f. on the same football team.
g. for one week.
h. a thorough investigation.
i. contribute money to war victims.
j. Mike Campbell's high school.

11. The warehouse guards . . . . . .   k. broke into the warehouse.
12. They testified that he . . . . . .   l. was overcrowded but clean.
13. Curtis' friends and neighbors . . .   m. pointed accusing fingers at Curtis.
14. The judge ordered . . . .   n. many notes.
15. The court recessed . . . .   o. from a Negro family.
16. Curtis stole to . . . .   p. maintained that he was a good boy.
17. The court was . . . .   q. Curtis' constitutional right.
18. Curtis was placed . . . .   r. he could for Curtis.

B.   1. Tell us what you know about a philanthropist.
     2. Describe circumstances in lower income households.
     3. Tell us what you think of Curtis Smith's action.
     4. Tell us what you think of Curtis' friends and neighbors.
     5. Tell us what you think of Curtis' friends at Euclid High.

C.   Describe what you see in the picture below.

D.   Read the poem aloud. Answer orally the questions listed following the poem.

The Boy with the Golden Hair. . .

The sweet smile that brightens[1] the dark of day,	[1] makes happy
the cry of joy when loved ones are at hand,[2]	[2] present
contentment[3] shining from the loving eyes. .	[3] pleasure
all these are part of the Boy with the golden hair. . .	
He falls, the guilt[4] and pain are mine,	[4] offense
for I was slow although my eyes perceived.[5]	[5] saw
Don't cry, my little star, my sweet little	
Boy with the golden hair. . :	
The grateful[6] touch of soft and precious[7] hands,	[6] thankful
the kiss of tiny lips upon a coarse[8] and manly cheek.	[7] wonderful
All these are mine—my image[9] he—and I the father of	[8] rough
the Boy with the golden hair. . .	[9] picture
And when at close of day a frown[10] is forced upon my brow	[10] sullen face
because of labors past and dreams still unfulfilled,[11]	[11] not done
but for this touch. .this smile. .this tear. .all's gone. .	
but he, the Boy with the golden hair. . .	

   1. Identify the *indefinite pronouns* in this poem.
   2. Identify all *adjectives* describing the boy.
   3. Identify the person speaking in the third stanza.
   4. What is the main idea here?

* * * * * *

Chapter Four

The Reluctant Ward

Words to remember:

Obligation with *should, ought, had better, have to*

Prepositions:
in, on, at, to

Possessive determiners:
*my, your, his, her,
its, our, your, their*

I. Narrative

A. Lori came to the adoptive agency under emotional and physical neglect. Because of the cruelty of her parents she was in custody of the agency. The agency made it known in a newspaper article that Lori was available for adoption. Mrs. Campbell answered the article. She called the welfare agency and asked to see Lori.

B. The first time she saw Lori, Mrs. Campbell knew she had better speak to the agent about her. The child was eight years old. Signs of abuse were evident. There was a large bruise under the girl's left eye. Lori's manners were different. She seemed more mature than most children eight years of age. Her large eyes had a look of sadness in them. Mrs. Campbell learned from the social worker that Lori had been unable to stay in two foster homes previously. They only increased her emotional problems.

C. Even though Lori was mistreated at home, she always returned there. Lori said that her little sister and her infant brother needed her. "The capacity to feel in Lori is extraordinary," said the social worker. "And she doesn't know about her illness, though it's terminal. This is also the reason for her lack of physical development." Mrs. Campbell said, "We'll do all we can for her when she comes to us."

D. Somehow, Lori remained withdrawn, full of tension and distrust toward the Campbell family. She refused food at first. Mrs. Campbell feared for Lori's health. The girl locked herself in her room for hours at a time. She ran away once. They found her wandering about in the neighborhood.

E. But love has a way of overcoming anxiety and distrust. The Campbell children were especially helpful. They treated their new sister with the same rough affection with which they treated one another. She was made to feel useful and needed. Gradually, she opened her heart to her new family.

F. Several months went by. One Sunday morning, Lori put her arms round her "mother's" neck affectionately. "I have to go home now," she said quietly. Mrs. Campbell looked at Lori with understanding. "Okay," she said. "Let's pack your things. We'll go after breakfast. But first we must get your things ready."

G. Mrs. Campbell helped Lori with her belongings. The sincerity of Lori's request did not disturb her. However, it was a difficult test for both of them, she knew. As they were leaving the house, Mrs. Campbell got the car keys off the hall table. Soon, they arrived at the old place where Lori used to live. Mrs. Campbell felt her pulse quicken.

H. The woman sat on the dirty sofa reading a newspaper. Lori ran toward the little girl who sat on the floor. "Linda! Linda!" Lori exclaimed excitedly. It was then the woman turned toward the visitors. The little girl approached her sister clumsily. She had a black eye. Lori kissed the little one affectionately. The woman became hysterical. She was about to attack Lori when Mrs. Campbell quickly interfered.

I. It was not until she was safe in the car that Lori spoke. "I love you, Mother Campbell." "I love you too, dear," Mrs. Campbell replied. "You know, Mother, I know we have to help them, but I guess there's no way we can do it." Lori didn't cry and she didn't complain. She was silent. "Who knows, darling, maybe you can help them after all," Mrs. Campbell said with a mysterious twinkle in her eyes. Lori moved closer to her mother. It was a good feeling.

* * *

II.   Words in Context   [Pictographs]

Below are the words used in the narrative. Where possible, each word has a [synonym]; or it is defined as used in the story. Where possible, an (*antonym*) is also given. Make up sentences about the pictographs choosing the words you need. Read aloud.

Example: (*calm*) = Lori was not calm.

A. B. and C.

Drawing of paragraph A, B & C

agency [department] ; abuse [maltreatment] (*care*); bruise [black and blue spot] ; cruel [brutal] (*gentle*); emotional [mental] (*calm*); evident [clear] (*concealed*); neglect [disregard] (*care*); physical [bodily] (*mental*); reluctant [hesitant] (*willing*); ward [adopted person] ; welfare [social service] ; manners [habitual or customary behavior] ; see [appear] (*conceal*); mature [grown up] (*immature*); sad [depressed] (*gay*); learn [be informed by] (*ignore*); social [public] (*personal*); foster [adopted] ; previous [prior] (*subsequent*); increase [grow] (*diminish*); problem [difficulty] (*solution*); mistreat [injure] (*care for*); return [come back] (*leave*); infant [child] (*adult*); capacity [skill] (*inability*); feel [be concerned] (*ignore*); extraordinary [remarkable] (*common*); illness [sickness] (*health*); terminal [fatal] (*curable*); lack [want] (*supply*); develop [grow] (*deteriorate*); face it [cope] (*avoid*)

D. and E.

Drawing of paragraph D & E

remain [continue] (*discontinue*); withdraw [retreat] (*emerge*); tension [anxiety] (*relaxation*); refuse [decline] (*accept*); fear [dread] (*trust*);

health [**well-being**] (*sickness*); lock [**confine**] (*open*); love [**affection**] (*hatred*); overcome [**conquer**] (*succumb to*); anxiety [**fear**] (*contentment*); distrust [**suspicion**] (*trust*); especially [**particularly**]; rough [**boisterous**] (*gentle*); useful [**helpful**] (*useless*); gradual [**step by step**] (*sudden*); open [**show her feelings**] (*become more withdrawn*); heart [**center of emotions**]; run away [**go away**] (*stay*); wander [**stroll about aimlessly**] (*walk purposefully*)

F. G. H. and I.

Drawing of paragraph F, G, H, & I

affectionate [**tender**] (*indifferent*); neck [**the part of man joining the head and body**]; reply [**answer**] (*ignore*); sincere [**honest**] (*feigned*); difficult [**hard**] (*easy*); leave [**depart**] (*return*); hall [**corridor**]; pulse [**heartbeat**]; quicken [**accelerate**] (*slow down*); dirty [**filthy**] (*clean*); sofa [**couch**]; excited [**enthusiastic**] (*passive*); clumsy [**awkward**] (*graceful*); speechless [**without words**] (*talkative*); hysterical [**uncontrolled**] (*calm*); quick [**prompt**] (*slow*); interference [**coming between**] (*not become involved*); attack [**assault**] (*aid*); until [**before**] (*afterward*); guess [**suppose**] (*be *certain*); cry [weep] (*laugh*); complain [whine] (*approve*); maybe [perhaps] (*impossible*); mysterious [secret] (*obvious*); twinkle [sparkle] (*be expressionless*); move [transfer] (*remain*)

III. Structures [Phrases]

Below are some phrases taken from the narrative. Make complete sentences and read them aloud.

A.	to	—	the	—	adoptive agency
B.	under	—	emotional	—	neglect
C.	because	—	of the	—	cruelty
D.	Lori	—	was	—	available
E.	was	—	in	—	custody
F.	made	—	it	—	known
G.	up	—	for	—	adoption
H.	the	—	first	—	time
I.	the	—	first	—	time
J.	speak	—	to	—	the agent
K.	was	—	eight years	—	old
L.	signs	—	of	—	abuse
M.	a	—	look	—	of sadness
N.	unable	—	to stay	—	in two
O.	mistreated	—	at	—	home
P.	sister and brother	—	needed	—	her
Q.	about	—	her	—	illness
R.	help	—	her	—	face it
S.	full	—	of	—	tension
T.	for	—	hours	—	at a time
U.	a way	—	of	—	overcoming
V.	like	—	to go	—	home
W.	they	—	were	—	leaving
X.	felt	—	her	—	pulse
Y.	toward	—	the	—	little
Z.	closer	—	to	—	her mother

IV. Sentences

A. Read the following sentences aloud. Repeat, substituting where possible, a synonym of the word in *italics,* or a phrase that explains the meaning.

Make other necessary changes.

Example: She was an *extraordinary* woman.
         She was a *remarkable* woman.

1. Because of her parents' *cruelty*, Lori was in custody.
2. The agency made it *known* in a newspaper article.
3. The child was *agitated*.
4. Signs of abuse were *evident*.
5. She was *reluctant* to stay in foster homes.
6. Lori always *returned* home.
7. Her *capacity* to feel was extraordinary.
8. She doesn't know about her *illness*.
9. Mrs. Campbell knew Lori's illness was *terminal*.
10. The Campbell children *remained* helpful.
11. Lori *withdrew* from everyone.
12. She *refused* to accept them.
13. Lori *feared* her real home.
14. Mrs. Campbell helped Lori to *overcome* fear.
15. Lori approached her little sister with *love*.
16. Mrs. Campbell *displayed* distrust toward the woman.
17. The woman wanted to *attack* her daughter.
18. Mrs. Campbell's reaction was *quick*.

B.   Fill in the blanks with words from the narrative. Each space may be filled
         by a word or phrase. Do not refer back to the narrative. Where possible,
         use variations of the missing words. Read aloud.

Lori came_____ the adoptive_____. She was _____ custody _____
the agency. They made it _____ a newspaper article that Lori was
_____ adoption. Mrs. Campbell knew she _____ speak
_____ the agent.

Signs_____ abuse were _____. Lori's _____ were different. She _____
more mature_____ most children eight years _____age. Her eyes had a
_____ sadness _____ them. Lori had been _____ stay
_____ two foster homes.

Even though Lori was _____ home, she always _____ there. "The
capacity_____ feel _____ Lori is_____ ," said the _____ worker. Mrs.
Campbell said, "We'll do_____ we can _____ her when she _____
us."

Lori refused_____ first. Mrs. Campbell feared _____ Lori's
        The girl_____herself_____her room for _____ a time.
She_____ once. She was wandering _____ the _____.
        Love has a _____ overcoming _____ and _____ . The children

were _____ helpful. Lori was made _____ feel _____ and _____ .

Several _____ went _____ . One _____ morning, Lori put _____ arms round _____ "mother's" neck. "I _____ go home now," she _____ . Mrs. Campbell looked _____ Lori with _____ .

Mrs. Campbell _____ Lori with _____ belongings. The _____ of Lori's _____ did not _____ her. It was a _____ test for both _____ them. They _____ at the old _____ where Lori used to _____ . Mrs. Campbell her pulse _____ .

The woman sat _____ the _____ sofa. Lori _____ toward the _____ girl. "Linda! Linda!" Lori exclaimed _____ . The woman turned _____ the visitors. The little _____ had a _____ eye. Lori _____ her sister _____ . The woman became _____ .

It was not _____ she was _____ in the car _____ Lori spoke. "I _____ you, Mother Campbell." Lori didn't _____ and she didn't _____ . She was _____ . She moved closer _____ mother. It was a _____ .

V. *Grammar and Syntax* *(Points of Interest)*

A. 1. When positive *obligation* or *advisability* is expressed, we use the words *should* or *ought*.

Mike *should* (or *ought* to) help his friend.

The helping verb we use here is *had better.*

When she saw Lori, Mrs. Campbell knew she *had better* speak to the agent.

2. *Have to + verb* means that *it is necessary* to do something.

"I *have to* go home now," Lori said.
"I know we *have* to help them," she said.

— —

B. **Prepositions** *in, on, at* and *to (toward)* answer the question *where (to)?*

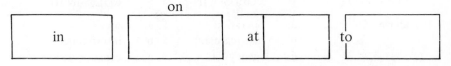

She was *in* custody of the agency.
They made it known *in* a newspaper article.

The little girl sat *on* the floor.
The woman sat *on* the sofa.

They arrived *at* the old place.
Lori was mistreated *at* home.

Lori came *to* the adoptive agency.
We'll do all we can for her when she comes *to* us.

She was full of tension and distrust *toward* the Campbell family.

[Other uses of prepositions are discussed elsewhere.]

— — — — — — — — — — — — — — — — —

C.   The *possessive determiner* [case] forms are:

I   — *my*   I have to help *my* little sister.
you   — *your*   *Your* child has a terminal illness.
he   — *his*   *His* mother came to visit.
she   — *her*   *Her* brother was abused.
it   — *its*   The child went on *its* way.
we   — *our*   We will treat her like *our* own.
you   — *your*   They say *your* mother is nice.
they — *their*   They treated *their* new sister well.

VI.   *Word Recognition*

A.   Circle the word (phrase) in Column II that is most *like* the word in Column I, and the word (phrase) in Column III most *unlike* the word in Column I. This oral identification of words ought to be timed.

COLUMN I		COLUMN II		COLUMN III
1. **abuse**	a.	operation	a.	break
	b.	maltreatment	b.	interference
	c.	agency	c.	care

2. **attack**
   - a. be quick
   - b. be prompt
   - c. assault

   - a. aid
   - b. interfere
   - c. come between

3. **clumsy**
   - a. speechless
   - b. awkward
   - c. without words

   - a. talkative
   - b. calm
   - c. graceful

4. **complain**
   - a. whine
   - b. care
   - c. approve

   - a. return
   - b. rejoice
   - c. want

5. **cruel**
   - a. brutal
   - b. bruised
   - c. broken

   - a. respected
   - b. gentle
   - c. healing

6. **difficult**
   - a. bad
   - b. good
   - c. hard

   - a. easy
   - b. quick
   - c. tough

7. **dirty**
   - a. filthy
   - b. bad
   - c. rough

   - a. open
   - b. free
   - c. clean

8. **distrust**
   - a. anxiety
   - b. eagerness
   - c. suspicion

   - a. contentment
   - b. trust
   - c. hatred

9. **evident**
   - a. gentle
   - b. brutal
   - c. clear

   - a. reluctant
   - b. concealed
   - c. unwilling

10. **gradual**
    - a. affectionate
    - b. slow
    - c. tender

    - a. sudden
    - b. indifferent
    - c. dishonest

11. **guess**
    - a. cry
    - b. suppose
    - c. weep

    - a. prove
    - b. laugh
    - c. complain

12. **infant**
    - a. child
    - b. nurse
    - c. boy

    - a. adult
    - b. grown-up
    - c. person

13. **lock**	a.	succumb to	a.	open
	b.	confine	b.	conquer
	c.	treat	c.	overcome
14. **mistreat**	a.	injure	a.	increase
	b.	diminish	b.	grow
	c.	doubt	c.	care for
15. **open**	a.	free	a.	worthless
	b.	helpful	b.	gradual
	c.	useful	c.	close
16. **previous**	a.	reluctant	a.	unwilling
	b.	prior	b.	agitated
	c.	emotional	c.	subsequent
17. **quick**	a.	fast	a.	aroused
	b.	hysterical	b.	slow
	c.	nice	c.	excited
18. **quicken**	a.	pulsate	a.	reply
	b.	accelerate	b.	answer
	c.	beat	c.	slow down
19. **refuse**	a.	dread	a.	trust
	b.	fear	b.	accept
	c.	reject	c.	heal
20. **remain**	a.	offer	a.	depart
	b.	stay	b.	come
	c.	want	c.	refuse
21. **rough**	a.	worthless	a.	helpful
	b.	slow	b.	gentle
	c.	boisterous	c.	useful
22. **sad**	a.	depressed	a.	mature
	b.	immature	b.	ripe
	c.	social	c.	gay

B.   In the space on the left write the word(s) that would best fit the expression in **bold print**. Make other necessary changes. Read aloud.

1. Lori came to the **adoptive** agency.

2. Signs of **improper treatment** were evident.

3. Her parents were **cruel**.

4. Lori was under **physical** neglect.

5. She was **reluctant** to stay in foster homes.

6. Lori's **manners** were different.

7. She seemed more **mature** than other children.

8. She looked **depressed**.

9. **Prior** to that she had stayed in two foster homes.

10. They increased her emotional **difficulties**.

11. The children were **injured**.

12. She always **came back** to her home.

13. Her **skill** to feel is extraordinary.

14. Her **sickness** is terminal.

15. This is the reason for the lack of **well-being**.

16. Lori **stayed** withdrawn.

17. **Love** overcomes anxiety.

18. The Campbell children were **particularly** helpful.

19. **Slowly**, she opened her heart.

20. Once she **strolled** through the neighborhood.

21. Lori was **tender** with Mrs. Campbell.

22. She **answered** quietly.

23. It was **hard** to understand.

24. She wanted to **depart** from home.

25. The woman became **uncontrolled**.

VIII. Concept Recognition

Fill in the most appropriate word (phrase) to express the CONCEPT of the sentence according to the narrative. Read the complete sentence aloud.

A. Because Lori was under_____ and_____ neglect, she came to the adoptive agency.

1. emotional, physical   2. uncertain, immaterial
3. calm, unwilling   4. reluctant, material

B. Lori was in custody because of the _____ of her parents.

1. gentleness   2. cruelty
3. welfare   4. ill luck

C. Lori was not like other girls, she had different _____ .

1. design   2. neglect
3. manners   4. problems

D. Lori left other foster homes because they _____ her emotional problems.

1. diminished   2. appeared
3. returned   4. increased

E. She returned home to _____ her little sister and brother.

1. help   2. develop
3. feel   4. increase

F. Her physical development was retarded because of the _____ illness.

1. temporary   2. prior
3. terminal   4. mature

G. Lori was mistreated, but her capacity to _____ was extraordinary.

1. supply   2. feel
3. develop   4. expand

H. Mrs. Campbell feared for Lori's health because the girl was _____ and _____ food.

1. withdrawn, refused   2. strained, relaxed
3. offered, accepted   4. expanded, dwarfed

I. When Lori ran away, they found her_____ about in the neighborhood.

1. wandering   2. succumbed
3. overcome   4. locked

J. The Campbell children were roughly affectionate to Lori, and this was _____ .

1. worthless
3. helpful
2. gradual
4. slow

K. In order to go home Lori had to _____ her things.

1. leave
3. pack
2. accelerate
4. return

L. Mrs. Campbell helped Lori because she _____ the girl.

1. ignored
3. loved
2. answered
4. replied

M. Lori was _____ when she saw her little sister.

1. excited
3. hysterical
2. uncontrolled
4. calm

N. Mrs. Campbell and Lori left the old house because the woman was about to _____ Lori.

1. love
3. twinkle
2. move
4. attack

VIII. Telling the Meaning

A. Place a check mark (✓) in front of the word in Column II that best fits the MEANING of the word in Column I. Read aloud a complete sentence using this word.

COLUMN I		COLUMN II
1. **accelerate**	_____ a.	quicken
	_____ b.	slow down
	_____ c.	pulsate
2. **affectionate**	_____ a.	tender
	_____ b.	indifferent
	_____ c.	difficult

3. **boisterous**

     _____ a.   gentle
     _____ b.   rough
     _____ c.   overcome

4. **brutal**

     _____ a.   cruel
     _____ b.   gentle
     _____ c.   emotional

5. **clear**

     _____ a.   uncertain
     _____ b.   evident
     _____ c.   calm

6. **confine**

     _____ a.   open
     _____ b.   lock
     _____ c.   love

7. **develop**

     _____ a.   grow
     _____ b.   dwarf
     _____ c.   avoid

8. **excited**

     _____ a.   aroused
     _____ b.   passive
     _____ c.   clumsy

9. **extraordinary**

     _____ a.   common
     _____ b.   examined
     _____ c.   remarkable

10. **fear**

     _____ a.   trust
     _____ b.   dread
     _____ c.   refuse

11. **filthy**

     _____ a.   excited
     _____ b.   dirty
     _____ c.   clean

12. **hysterical**

     _____ a.   uncontrolled
     _____ b.   calm
     _____ c.   sweet

13. **increase**

     _____ a.   diminish
     _____ b.   grow
     _____ c.   doubt

14. **interference**   _____ a.   not become involved
                        _____ b.   come between
                        _____ c.   safety

15. **lack**   _____ a.   want
                        _____ b.   supply
                        _____ c.   develop

16. **maltreatment**   _____ a.   respect
                        _____ b.   doubt
                        _____ c.   abuse

17. **mysterious**   _____ a.   willing
                        _____ b.   obvious
                        _____ c.   secret

18. **physical**   _____ a.   distant
                        _____ b.   bodily
                        _____ c.   emotional

19. **reluctant**   _____ a.   unwilling
                        _____ b.   willing
                        _____ c.   brutal

20. **remain**   _____ a.   stay
                        _____ b.   depart
                        _____ c.   return

21. **return**   _____ a.   come back
                        _____ b.   leave
                        _____ c.   feel

22. **sincere**   _____ a.   feigned
                        _____ b.   hard
                        _____ c.   honest

23. **social**   _____ a.   personal
                        _____ b.   public
                        _____ c.   previous

24. **terminal**   _____ a.   curable
                        _____ b.   temporary
                        _____ c.   fatal

25. **useful**   _____ a.   useless
                                                  _____ b.   helpful
                                                  _____ c.   gradual

B.   Return to Exercise A. Place two check marks (✓✓) in front of the word in
      COLUMN II that is the ANTONYM of the word in COLUMN I. Read
      aloud a complete sentence using this word.

C.   Select one of the three (3) words (phrases) that best fulfills the MEANING
      of the sentence according to the narrative. Insert the word in the blank
      space. Read the completed sentence aloud.

  1. Lori was at the adoptive agency because she was_____ at home.
      a. mistreated   b. calm   c. uncontrolled

  2. Mrs. Campbell wanted to adopt Lori so that she could_____ her.
      a. respect   b. help   c. neglect

  3. Lori's manners were different because she seemed more_____ .
      a. mature   b. gentle   c. material

  4. Mrs. Campbell learned about Lori's_____ from the social worker.
      a. mature feeling   b. emotional   c. sister
                                    problems

  5. Lori always returned home to_____ her sister and brother.
      a. help   b. supply   c. ignore

  6. Because of her experience, Lori had an _____ to feel.
      a. sad certainty   b. doubt problem   c. extraordinary
                                                          capacity

  7. Lori distrusted the Campbells and remained_____ .
      a. withdrawn   b. relaxed   c. gay

  8. The Campbells loved her and Lori_____ her_____ and distrust.
      a. ignored, fear   b. overcame, anxiety   c. doubt, problem

  9. When Lori wanted to go home, Mrs. Campbell _____ she would lose
      her.
      a. appeared   b. wanted   c. feared

10. When the woman became_____, Lori knew her home was with the Campbells.
    a. hysterical   b. extraordinary   c. affectionate

IX. *Comprehension   [Exercises]*

A. Place a check mark (✓) in front of the correct response to each of the following statements according to the narrative. Read the complete sentence aloud.

1. Lori was in custody of the agency because

    _____ a. she was a child of eleven.
    _____ b. of the cruelty of her parents.
    _____ c. she liked her sister.

2. A newspaper article made it known that

    _____ a. Lori was up for adoption.
    _____ b. Lori was ill.
    _____ c. Lori was at the Campbells.

3. Mrs. Campbell learned about Lori from

    _____ a. her neighbors.
    _____ b. the agency.
    _____ c. the newspaper.

4. Lori's manners were different because

    _____ a. she was a girl.
    _____ b. she seemed more mature.
    _____ c. she was depressed.

5. Lori always returned to her home

    _____ a. to see her mother.
    _____ b. to run away.
    _____ c. to help her little sister and brother.

6. Lori lacked physical development because

    _____ a. of her illness.
    _____ b. of her inability to feel.
    _____ c. of her want.

7. The Campbells were kind to Lori because

_____ a. they loved her.
_____ b. they needed her.
_____ c. they played with her.

8. The Campbell children helped Lori

_____ a. with her housework.
_____ b. overcome her anxiety and distrust.
_____ c. with her family.

9. When Mrs. Campbell took Lori home, she

_____ a. cried.
_____ b. packed her things.
_____ c. was afraid.

10. Mrs. Campbell knew it was going to be

_____ a. a difficult test for both of them.
_____ b. a nice ride to town.
_____ c. a remarkable experience.

11. When Lori saw Linda she was

_____ a. very depressed.
_____ b. very excited.
_____ c. very ill.

12. When the woman saw Lori

_____ a. she got very depressed.
_____ b. she got hysterical.
_____ c. she was happy.

13. On the way back to the Campbells

_____ a. Lori didn't cry.
_____ b. Lori cried.
_____ c. Lori was very neglected.

14. Lori wished she could

_____ a. stay with her mother.
_____ b. stay with the Campbells.
_____ c. help her brother and sister.

15. When Lori moved closer to Mrs. Campbell,

    _____ a. it was rough.
    _____ b. it was a good feeling.
    _____ c. it was a twinkle.

B.   Below there are three (3) different thoughts expressed in each of the exercises. Assign the proper sequence (order) of THOUGHT, according to the narrative, by numbering 1 to 3. Read aloud.

1. a. in a newspaper article   _____
   b. the agency made it known   _____
   c. that Lori was up for adoption   _____

2. a. in custody of the agency   _____
   b. of her parents, she was   _____
   c. because of the cruelty   _____

3. a. and asked to see Lori   _____
   b. the welfare agency   _____
   c. she called   _____

4. a. speak to the agent about her   _____
   b. the first time she saw Lori   _____
   c. Mrs. Campbell knew she had better   _____

5. a. eight years of age   _____
   b. mature than most children   _____
   c. she seemed more   _____

6. a. sadness in them   _____
   b. had a look of   _____
   c. her large eyes   _____

7. a. she always returned there   _____
   b. was mistreated at home   _____
   c. even though Lori   _____

8. a. when she comes to us   _____
   b. we can for her   _____
   c. we'll do all   _____

9. a. for hours at a time   _____
   b. in her room   _____
   c. the girl locked herself   _____

10. a. they treated one another   _____
    b. the same rough affection with which   _____
    c. they treated their new sister with   _____

11. a. ready after breakfast   _____
    b. as you have things   _____
    c. we'll go as soon   _____

12. a. as they were leaving the house,   _____
    b. the car keys off the hall table   _____
    c. Mrs. Campbell got   _____

13. a. where Lori used to live   _____
    b. soon they arrived   _____
    c. at the old place   _____

14. a. reading a newspaper   _____
    b. the woman sat   _____
    c. on the dirty sofa   _____

15. a. that Lori spoke   _____
    b. it was not until   _____
    c. she was safe in the car   _____

16. a. help them after all   _____
    b. who knows, my child,   _____
    c. maybe you can   _____

C.   There are some statements listed below about the narrative. Write **T** for **True** in front of each statement that you think is true. Write **F** for **False** if the statement is not true. Read aloud.

_____ 1. Lori came to the adoptive agency calmly.

_____ 2. She was in custody because of the cruelty of her parents.

_____ 3. Mrs. Campbell learned about Lori from a newspaper article.

_____ 4. When Mrs. Campbell saw Lori there was a large bruise under her eye.

_____ 5. Lori's manners were like most children her age.

_____ 6. Lori seemed more mature than most children her age.

_____ 7. Her large eyes had a happy look.

_____ 8. Lori stayed in four foster homes.

_____ 9. Lori returned to her home because she was treated well.

_____ 10. Lori had a common capacity to feel.

_____ 11. Lori had a temporary illness.

_____ 12. At first Lori remained withdrawn.

_____ 13. She ate well at first.

_____ 14. Mrs. Campbell had trust in Lori's health.

_____ 15. Lori ran away once.

_____ 16. The Campbell children treated Lori like one of them.

_____ 17. They made her feel useless.

_____ 18. One Sunday morning Lori asked to be taken home.

_____ 19. Mrs. Campbell told Lori not to go.

_____ 20. The woman reading the paper was Lori's mother.

_____ 21. The woman was calm when she saw Lori.

_____ 22. When they left, Lori cried and complained.

_____ 23. Mrs. Campbell was affectionate with Lori.

X.   *Composition and Discussion*

A.   In COLUMN I are the beginnings of sentences. In COLUMN II are the completions to sentences of COLUMN I. Select the completion best fitting each sentence in COLUMN I according to the narrative. Read the completed sentences orally. Compose new sentences orally and discuss the narrative.

COLUMN I	COLUMN II
1. Lori came to the adoptive agency .	a. she always returned there.
2. Because of the cruelty of her parents	b. than most children eight years of age.
3. Mrs. Campbell called	c. for her when she comes to us.
4. The child was	d. under emotional and physical neglect.
5. Signs of abuse	e. in Lori was extraordinary.

6. She seemed more mature . . . . .   f. of overcoming anxiety and distrust.
7. Her large eyes had . . . .   g. were especially helpful.
8. Even though Lori was mistreated
   at home . . . .   h. her heart to her new family.
9. The capacity to feel . . . .   i. were evident.
10. We'll do all we can   . . . .   j. for Lori's health.
11. She refused food   . . . .   k. she was in the custody of the
                                               agency.
12. Mrs. Campbell feared . . . . . .   l. at first.
13. They found her wandering . . . .   m. little girl who sat on the floor.
14. But love had a way . . . .   n. with her belongings.
15. The Campbell children . . . . . .   o. reading a newspaper.
16. Gradually, she opened . . . . . .   p. a look of sadness in them.
17. Mrs. Campbell helped Lori . . . .   q. about in the neighborhood.
18. The woman sat on the dirty sofa. .   r. the welfare agency.
19. Lori ran toward the . . . .   s. eight years old.

B.　　1. Tell us what you know about Lori.
　　　　2. Tell us about Lori's family.
　　　　3. What do you know about a welfare agency?
　　　　4. How did the Campbell family accept Lori?
　　　　5. Describe Lori's visit to her old home.

C.　　Describe what you see in the picture below.

D. Read the poem aloud. Answer orally the questions listed following the poem.

Hospitality[1]   [1] cordiality

The soul,[2] *and then into*   [2] spirit
the smallest recesses[3]   [3] niche
of my heart came
the ineffable[4] *feeling*   [4] inexpressible
of happiness. .

Can it cease[5] *to exist*   [5] stop
because of mere
mortality?[6] *Then*   [6] death

should we be destined[7]   [7] fated
to meet there
at the crossroads of
our life-span,[8]   [8] lifetime

if I were first,
or you, or both
we were together,

do again, as you
have done before!
The memory[9] *of joy*   [9] recollection
will stay. .mine. .
perhaps forevermore. . ?

   1. Identify all *possessive determiners.*
   2. Identify all *prepositions.*
   3. Which stanza expresses happiness? Why?
   4. What wish is expressed in the last stanza?

* * * * * *

Chapter Five

The Would-Be President

Words to remember:

Present perfect tense
have + past participle

Future time:
will, I'll or *shall + infinitive*

request—question

Possessive pronouns:
*mine, yours, his, hers, its
ours, yours, theirs*

place:	*where?*
manner:	*how?*
time:	*when?*

I.   Narrative

A.   Mike has never been this excited before. He came home from school earlier than usual. "Mom!" he yelled. "I'm running for president of our student council!" Mrs. Campbell sensed something unusual in her son's behavior. "Let's have a cola, Mike," she suggested, "and you can tell me all about it."

B.   They sat at the table. Mike told her that he has been asked by the student council president to run. "I think they had a wide choice of candidates. But they selected me. They think I'll surely win." "I'm glad they want you, Mike. But don't be too sure of yourself," Mrs. Campbell cautioned. "There are four other candidates, but I'm sure I have a good chance to win," Mike repeated. He was excited.

C.   From the moment his name has been placed on the ballot, Mike was constantly on a merry-go-round. "You should go to bed earlier," Mrs. Campbell would tell her son. "You haven't eaten supper with your family lately," Mr. Campbell remarked. "I would slow down if I could, dad. But this is important. Things progress fast. I can't let my opponents get ahead of me," Mike replied to the admonishments of his parents. "Anyway, I will rest when it's all over, I promise," he added with a smile.

D.   "If only he would dress this way all the time," Mrs. Campbell said at breakfast time. A complete change has come over Mike's dressing habits. Coat and tie were his daily attire during the campaign. In the past, he would never be seen in a tie at school. "I'll impress people as a neat dresser," he said, noticing the puzzled looks around the breakfast table. "Will I win the election, father?" Mike asked suddenly. "I'll prepare a good speech. Will you listen to it?" "Of course, son, we will all listen to your speech. Then if you can convince us, you'll convince your fellow students." Mr. Campbell knew how to encourage Mike.

E.   The election day came. It hasn't been easy for Mike to prepare his speech. "Yours is the best speech I've heard in years!" Mrs. Campbell exclaimed. "It may sound good here, but wait till I stand on the stage, in front of the entire student body. My teeth will be making so much noise, you won't be able to hear what I say!" Mike was really concerned. "You'll say it forcefully, Mike, the way it should be said," Mr. Campbell said. "I can hardly wait to hear it." Mrs. Campbell remarked, "I'll be at school tomorrow to listen."

F.   Mrs. Campbell proudly listened to her son's words. "Each president must dutifully maintain a working communication between the students and the administration," Mike stated. "We have a good school here," he continued. "With the cooperation of a concerned administration we should be able to accomplish a common goal in the upcoming school year. If our requests are sensible, I'm sure that the response will likewise be sensible." Mike paused.

G. "I say to you that I am aware of my responsibilities and shall be fully accountable for my actions to you. If I am elected, the student council will strive to achieve common goals with the administration. This, I pledge to you. Thank you."

H. Mike finished his election speech. There was applause. Someone asked Mrs. Campbell, "Was that your son?" "Yes, that's my son!" Mrs. Campbell proudly replied. The friend said, "He delivered a fine speech. I hope he'll win." "So do I," Mrs. Campbell said.

I. It was not as the Campbells had wished. The following day, Mike returned home looking sad. "And he wasn't even the best man!" he exclaimed. "My speech was better than any of theirs!" Mike was close to tears. "You shouldn't take it this hard, Mike," Mr. Campbell said. "Think of how much you've learned from it." "Still," Mike insisted, "I can't help thinking that something is wrong when candidates get elected on popularity rather than on qualifications." "The students voted, Mike. The vote is the voice of the people in our system," Mr. Campbell added. "Well, I don't agree with the way elections are held," Mike said stubbornly. "Some day, I'll work to change that."

* * *

II.   *Words in Context*   *[Pictographs]*

Below are some of the words used in the narrative. Where possible, each word has a **[synonym]**, or it is defined as used in the story. Where possible, an (*antonym*) is also given. Make up sentences about the pictographs choosing the words you need. Read aloud.

Example: (*council*) = Mike was selected by the student council.

A. and B.

council **[planning body]**; sense **[feel]** (*ignore*); good behavior **[good conduct]** (*misbehavior*); suggest **[hint]** (*declare*); wide **[broad]** (*narrow*); choice **[many to pick from]** (*limited selection*); candidate **[nominee]**; select **[pick]** (*ignore, overlook*); sure **[certain]** (*uncertain*); caution **[warn]** (*disregard*); win **[get]** (*lose*)

C. and D.

ballot **[voting sheet]**; constant **[always]** (*seldom*); lately **[recently]** (*long ago*); remark **[notice]** (*disregard*); slow down **[ease up]** (*speed up*); important **[significant]** (*insignificant*); let **[allow]** (*refuse*); opponent

Drawing marked A. and B.

[**adversary**] (*friend*); get ahead [**progress**] (*fall behind*); admonish [**warn**];
dress [**clothe**] (*undress*); complete [**total**] (*incomplete*); habit [**custom**];
attire [**dress**] (*bareness*); impress [**affect**] (*unimpress*); notice [**pay
attention**] (*ignore*); prepare [**fix**]; convince [**persuade**] (*dissuade*); encourage [**support**] (*discourage*)

E., F. and G.

sound [**seem**]; in front of [**before**] (*behind*); entire [**whole**] (*partial*);
noise [**clamor**] (*stillness*); concerned [**nervous**] (*indifferent*); forceful
[**powerful**] (*weak*); proudly [**with pride**] (*humbly*); duty [**responsibility**]
(*freedom*); maintain [**keep**] (*drop*); communicate [**exchange ideas**];
continue [**persist**] (*cease*); cooperate [**work together**] (*oppose*);
accomplish [**achieve**] (*give up*); request [**proposal**] (*command*); conscious
of [**realistic**] (*unrealistic*); response [**reply**]; likewise [**also**] (*otherwise*);
aware [**sensible**] (*unaware*); accountable [**responsible**] (*irresponsible*);
strive [**labor**] (*loaf*); achieve [**accomplish**] (*fail*); pledge [**promise**] (*refuse*)

Drawing of paragraph C & D

H. and I.

finish [**end**] (*start*); applause [**acclamation**] ; deliver [**give**] (*take*); fine [**good**] (*bad*); close [**near**] (*far*); hard [**difficult to bear**] (*easygoing*); insist [**maintain**] (*yield*); popular [**favorite**] (*unpopular*); qualification [**capability**] (*inability*); system [**method**] (*disorder*); stubborn [**obstinate**] (*docile*); change [**alter**] (*retain*)

III. Structures   *[Phrases]*

Below are some phrases taken from the narrative. Make complete sentences and read them aloud.

A.	never	—	this	—	excited
B.	home	—	from	—	school
C.	earlier	—	than	—	usual

Drawing of paragraph E, F & G

D.	for	—	president		
E.	something	—	unusual		
F.	all	—	about	—	it
G.	at	—	the	—	table
H.	by	—	the	—	student council
I.	a	—	wide	—	choice
J.	too	—	sure	—	of yourself
K.	four	—	other	—	candidates
L.	a	—	good	—	chance
M.	red	—	with	—	excitement
N.	on	—	a	—	merry-go-round
O.	with	—	your	—	family
P.	opponents	—	get	—	ahead
Q.	of	—	his	—	parents
R.	at	—	breakfast	—	time
S.	his	—	daily	—	attire
T.	during	—	the	—	campaign
U.	impress	—	people		

Drawing of paragraph H & I

V.	puzzled	—	looks	—	round the table
W.	best	—	speech	—	in years
X.	it	—	may	—	sound good
Y.	stand	—	on	—	the stage
Z.	in	—	front of	—	the entire

IV. Sentences

A. Read the following sentences aloud. Repeat, substituting where possible, the synomym of the word in *italics,* or a phrase that explains the meaning. Make other necessary changes.

Example: His *conduct* changed.
         His *behavior* was different.

1. We will proceed with *care.*
2. You won't hear any *noise.*

3. Mike was really *concerned.*
4. You'll say it *forcefully.*
5. Mrs. Campbell *proudly* listened to Mike's words.
6. We should be able to *accomplish* a common goal.
7. The *response* will be sensible.
8. I am aware of my *duties.*
9. I shall be *accountable* for my actions.
10. I *pledge* this to you.
11. Mike *finished* his election speech.
12. He *delivered* a fine speech.
13. Mike was *close* to tears.
14. It was *hard* to lose.
15. Mike *maintained* that something was wrong.
16. The students voted for their *favorite* candidate.
17. The *method* of voting was wrong.
18. Some day I'll work to *change* that.

B. Fill in the blanks with words from the narrative. Each space may be filled by a word or phrase. Do not refer back to the narrative. Where possible, use variations of the missing words. Read aloud.

Mike _____ never _____ this excited _____ . "I'm _____ for president!" he _____. Mrs. Campbell _____ something _____ . _____

They _____ at the table. Mike _____ her that he _____ asked to _____ . They had a _____ choice of _____ . But they _____ Mike. "I have a _____ chance to _____ ," Mike _____ .

His name _____ placed on the _____ . Mike was on a _____ . His mother told him to slow _____ . "I can't _____ my _____ get _____ of me," Mike _____ . I will _____ when it's all _____ ."

"If only he _____ dress this way _____ the _____ ," Mrs. Campbell _____ . A _____ change had come over Mike's _____ habits. In the _____ he _____ never _____ in a tie at _____ . "I'll _____ a good _____ ," Mike said. "If you _____ us, you'll convince your _____ students."

The _____ day came. It _____ been _____ for Mike. "Wait till I _____ on the _____ in front of the _____ student body!" Mike was _____ . "You _____ say it _____ ," Mr. Campbell said. "I can _____ wait to _____ it," Mrs. Campbell remarked.

Mrs. Campbell _____ listened to her _____ speech. "We have a good _____ ," Mike said. "We should be _____ to _____ a common goal in the _____ school year. If our _____ are _____ , I'm sure that the _____ will be _____ sensible."

"I am _____ of my _____ and shall be _____ for my _____ to you. If I am _____ , we'll strive to _____ common goals with the _____ ."

Mike _____ his _____ speech. There was _____.

The _____ day, Mike _____ home looking _____. "My speech was _____ than any of _____." "You shouldn't _____ it this _____, Mike," Mrs. Campbell said. "Think of how much you _____ learned from it." "The students _____, Mike. The _____ is the _____ of the _____ in our _____," Mr. Campbell added.

V. *Grammar and Syntax* *[Points of Interest]*

A. The **Present Perfect** states something in the past that exists at the time of speaking. To form the *present perfect* we use the verb *have + past participle.*

Mike *has been asked* to run.
You *haven't eaten* supper with your family lately.
It *hasn't been* easy for Mike.
Think how much *you've learned* from it.

_ _ _ _ _ _ _ _ _ _ _ _ _ _ _ _ _ _ _ _

B. **Future Time** *will, I'll* or *shall* + infinitive

There is no verb to form the future tense as there was for the past tense. We will use the verb *will, 'll,* or *shall* to express the future. This form also expresses

1. *willingness,* or a *promise,* or an *agreement* with someone:

Some day, I *'ll work* to change that.
I *'ll* (I *will*) *impress* the people.
I *'ll* (I *will*) *prepare* a good speech.

2. *request:*

Will you *listen* to it?
Will you please *slow* down?

3. *questions* about the *future:*

Will I *win* the election?
Will you *help* me?

_ _ _ _ _ _ _ _ _ _ _ _ _ _ _ _ _ _ _ _

C. **Possessive Pronouns** are used in place of both a *possessive determiner* and a *noun*.

my son	=	*mine*	its son	=	*its*
your son	=	*yours*	our son	=	*ours*
his son	=	*his*	your son	=	*yours*
her son	=	*hers*	their son	=	*theirs*

> Was *my* speech good?
> *Yours* was the best.
> Yes, *mine* was better than *theirs.*

— — — — — — — — — — — — — — — — — —

D. **Adverbials** answer the question words **[interrogatives]** *where?* (place), *how?* (manner), *when?* (time) of an action. *Adverbs* are the most common adverbials.

1. Place **[where?]**

> They sat *at the table.*
> He never wore a tie *at school.*
> It sounds good *here.*
> It will be different *on the stage.*
> We have a good school *here.*

2. Manner **[how?]**

> Most *adverbs of manner* are words that describe.

> (adjectives) + *-ly*

> You haven't eaten supper with your family *lately.*
> Mike dressed *neatly* during elections.
> I can *hardly* wait to hear it.
> Mrs. Campbell *proudly* listened.

> Some adverbs of *manner* have no ending *-ly.*

> Things progress *fast.*

3. Time **[when?]**

> The adverb of *time* is usually last, but it can begin a sentence when there is more than one adverb present.

TIME	PLACE	MANNER
Tomorrow	on the freeway	he'll drive slowly.

Last night   at school   he spoke carefully.

- - - - - - - - - - - - - - - - - - - -

E.   Uses of Modal Auxiliaries

1.   We have used the auxiliary *would* in the sense of *be willing to.*
      If only he *would* dress this way all the time.

2.   We have used the auxiliary *should* to express

   a.   *advisability:*
         You *should* go to bed earlier.
         You *shouldn't* take it this hard.

   b.   *expectation:*
         We *should* be able to accomplish a common end.

VI.   *Word Recognition*

A.   Circle the word (phrase) in Column II most *like* the word in Column I, and
          the word (phrase) in Column III most *unlike* the word in Column I. This
          oral identification of words ought to be timed.

	COLUMN I		COLUMN II		COLUMN III
1.	**accomplish**	a.	achieve	a.	fail
		b.	maintain	b.	demand
		c.	sustain	c.	think
2.	**concerned**	a.	forceful	a.	humble
		b.	nervous	b.	indifferent
		c.	powerful	c.	weak
3.	**duty**	a.	responsibility	a.	choice
		b.	behavior	b.	attire
		c.	labor	c.	freedom
4.	**finish**	a.	deliver	a.	confine
		b.	end	b.	start
		c.	liberate	c.	fine
5.	**get ahead**	a.	progress faster	a.	fall behind

	b.	prepare	b.	admonish
	c.	fix	c.	warn

6. **hard**
   a. difficult to bear a. easygoing
   b. insistent b. sensible
   c. persistent c. bad

7. **impress**
   a. notice a. unimpress
   b. mark b. neglect
   c. affect c. undress

8. **let**
   a. ease up a. refuse
   b. be quick b. be glad
   c. allow c. be pleased

9. **place**
   a. put a. win
   b. suggest b. remove
   c. hint c. declare

10. **popular**
    a. right a. unpopular
    b. firm b. bad
    c. favorite c. wrong

11. **qualification**
    a. system a. incapability
    b. capability b. disorder
    c. method c. coarseness

12. **rest**
    a. complete a. work
    b. repose b. dress
    c. accomplish c. clothe

13. **select**
    a. elect a. get ahead
    b. ballot b. abandon
    c. let c. allow

14. **sense**
    a. feel a. ignore
    b. plan b. misbehave
    c. gather c. conduct

15. **suddenly**
    a. slowly a. gradually
    b. abruptly b. well
    c. fast c. sensible

16. **suggest**
    a. hint a. allow

b.	caution	b.	declare
c.	care	c.	give

17. **wide** a. small a. bad
  b. good b. narrow
  c. broad c. concerned

B. In the space on the left write the word(s) that best fit the expression in **bold print**. Make other necessary changes. Read aloud.

_____ 1. Mrs. Campbell sensed something unusual in her son's **conduct**.

_____ 2. They had a wide **option** of candidates.

_____ 3. They **elected** me.

_____ 4. I think I'll **certainly** win.

_____ 5. I'm **pleased** they want you.

_____ 6. His name has been **put** on the ballot.

_____ 7. You haven't eaten your **evening meal**.

_____ 8. I would **ease up** if I could.

_____ 9. This is **pressing**.

_____ 10. I can't **permit** my **adversary** to get ahead.

_____ 11. His parents **warned** him.

_____ 12. A change came over his dressing **customs**.

_____ 13. Mike asked his father **abruptly**.

_____ 14. If you **persuade** us you'll persuade them.

_____ 15. Mrs. Campbell knew how to **support** Mike.

_____ 16. He stood in front of the **whole** student body.

_____ 17. It is our **obligation** to communicate.

_____ 18. Our **demands** are sensible.

_____ 19. The **reply** will be **also** sensible.

_____ 20. I will **labor** to **gain** the goals.

_____ 21. He **rendered** a fine speech.

_____ 22. He looked **sorrowful**.

_____ 23. I want to get elected on my **capability**.

_____ 24. This election **method** is wrong.

_____ 25. Mike was **obstinate**.

VII. *Concept Recognition*

Fill in the most appropriate word (phrase) to express the CONCEPT of the sentence according to the narrative. Read the complete sentence aloud.

A. Mike came home earlier than usual because he was _____ for president of the student body.

1. yelling	2. going
3. running	4. having

B. Mrs. Campbell suggested a cola because she _____ .

1. sensed something unusual	2. liked a drink
3. was in a hurry	4. Mike was sad

C. Mike was glad that he was the _____ of the student council.

1. president	2. student
3. choice	4. name

D. Mike was sure he'd win, but Mrs. Campbell _____ him.

1. reassured	2. cautioned
3. excited	4. reminded

E. Mike was on a merry-go-round because things _____ .

1. slow down	2. are important
3. go well	4. progressed fast

F. Mike refused to listen to his parents' admonishments saying he'd rest when _____ .

1. it's all over	2. he loses the election
3. he wins the election	4. his opponent wins

G.   The candidate dressed in coat and tie to_____ the students.

    1. notice   2. change
    3. impress   4. campaign

H.   Mike prepared a good _____ to _____ the students.

    1. dress, please   2. speech, convince
    3. quiz, ask   4. dinner, win

I.   Everyone in the Campbell family_____ Mike.

    1. liked   2. prepared
    3. convinced   4. encouraged

J.   Mike worked hard on his speech to _____ the election.

    1. win   2. convince
    3. prepare   4. complete

K.   Mike said in his speech that there must be _____ between the students
and administration.

    1. election   2. work
    3. communication   4. continuation

L.   A common end can be accomplished if the administration is _____.

    1. common   2. concerned
    3. upcoming   4. able

M.   Only_____ requests bring _____ response.

    1. good, better   2. sensible, sensible
    3. common, upcoming   4. concerned, common

N.   Mike was sad because he lost, and he thought _____ .

    1. he was a better   2. no candidate was good
       candidate
    3. the other candidate   4. he didn't speak well
       was better

O.   Mike thought the system of electing candidates on _____ rather than on
qualifications was _____ .

    1. popularity, wrong   2. work, good
    3. cooperation, right   4. dressing, wrong

VIII. *Telling the Meaning*

A. Place a check mark (✓) in front of the word in COLUMN II that best fits the MEANING of the word in COLUMN I. Read aloud a complete sentence using this word.

COLUMN I   COLUMN II

1. **abruptly**   _____ a.   suddenly
                          _____ b.   gradually
                          _____ c.   promptly

2. **accident**   _____ a.   caution
                          _____ b.   chance
                          _____ c.   plan

3. **accountable**   _____ a.   weak
                          _____ b.   responsible
                          _____ c.   irresponsible

4. **achieve**   _____ a.   give up
                          _____ b.   accomplish
                          _____ c.   cooperate

5. **affect**   _____ a.   notice
                          _____ b.   impress
                          _____ c.   unimpress

6. **capability**   _____ a.   method
                          _____ b.   incapability
                          _____ c.   qualification

7. **caution**   _____ a.   care
                          _____ b.   ability
                          _____ c.   recklessness

8. **complete**   _____ a.   incomplete
                          _____ b.   total
                          _____ c.   sensible

9. **concerned**   _____ a.   indifferent
                          _____ b.   nervous
                          _____ c.   sensible

10. **constant**
    _____ a. accountable
    _____ b. always
    _____ c. seldom

11. **convince**
    _____ a. dissuade
    _____ b. persuade
    _____ c. encourage

12. **early**
    _____ a. soon
    _____ b. late
    _____ c. wide

13. **front**
    _____ a. face
    _____ b. back
    _____ c. part

14. **get ahead**
    _____ a. progress faster
    _____ b. get behind
    _____ c. admonish

15. **hint**
    _____ a. say
    _____ b. declare
    _____ c. suggest

16. **important**
    _____ a. significant
    _____ b. unimportant
    _____ c. complete

17. **likewise**
    _____ a. also
    _____ b. otherwise
    _____ c. important

18. **maintain**
    _____ a. keep
    _____ b. drop
    _____ c. communicate

19. **note**
    _____ a. remark
    _____ b. disregard
    _____ c. remove

20. **opponent**
    _____ a. adversary
    _____ b. friend
    _____ c. caution

21. **permit**
    _____ a. change
    _____ b. refuse
    _____ c. let

22. **put**
    _____ a. remove
    _____ b. place
    _____ c. lose

23. **responsibility**
    _____ a. duty
    _____ b. freedom
    _____ c. command

24. **slow down**
    _____ a. speed up
    _____ b. ease up
    _____ c. press

25. **sure**
    _____ a. certain
    _____ b. important
    _____ c. uncertain

B. Return to Exercise A. Place two check marks (✓) in front of the word in COLUMN II that is the ANTONYM of the word in COLUMN I. Read aloud a complete sentence using this word.

C. Select one of the three (3) words (phrases) that best fulfills the MEANING of the sentence according to the narrative. Insert the word in the blank space.

   1. Mike was was excited because he was _____ for president of the student body.
      a. running   b. voting   c. unusual

   2. The student council had a wide choice of candidates, but they _____ Mike.
      a. told   b. selected   c. repeated

   3. Mike was sure of winning, but Mrs. Campbell _____ him.
      a. excited   b. selected   c. cautioned

   4. When he ran for president, Mike was constantly _____ .
      a. on a merry-go-round   b. excited   c. slow

   5. Mike could not _____ because things _____ fast.

a. slow down,   b. understand it,   c. rest well,
   progressed   got   went

6. Mike promised to _____ when it was all over.
   a. vote   b. smile   c. rest

7. He dressed in coat and tie to _____ people.
   a. see   b. impress   c. win

8. The Campbells listened to Mike's speech to see if he could _____ them.
   a. fool   b. tell   c. convince

9. Mr. Campbell said a speech should be done _____.
   a. forcefully   b. concerned   c. easy

10. To accomplish a common goal, the requests should be _____.
    a. good   b. common   c. sensible

11. When Mike returned home he was sad because he _____.
    a. wasn't the best man   b. was a better man   c. he didn't win
                             than his opponent

IX.   Comprehension   *[Exercises]*

A.   Place a check mark (✓) in front of the correct response to each of the statements according to the narrative. Read the complete sentences aloud.

1. Mike was excited because

   ____ a. he was elected president.
   ____ b. he was running for president.
   ____ c. he came home earlier than usual.

2. Mrs. Campbell suggested a cola to

   ____ a. learn more abut Mike's candidacy.
   ____ b. practice Mike's speech.
   ____ c. make a speech.

3. Mike was glad that he was

   ____ a. having a cola.

___ b. talking to his mother.

___ c. selected out of a wide choice of candidates.

4. Mike was sure

___ a. he had a good chance to win.

___ b. he would win.

___ c. he wouldn't win.

5. Mike could not slow down because

___ a. his opponents were ahead of him.

___ b. things progressed fast.

___ c. his parents admonished him.

6. Mike promised to slow down when

___ a. he won the election.

___ b. ate supper.

___ c. it was all over.

7. Mike dressed in coat and tie to

___ a. win the election.

___ b. impress people.

___ c. make a complete change.

8. It was important for Mike to prepare a good speech to

___ a. convince his fellow students.

___ b. convince his family.

___ c. convince himself.

9. Mike thought he would be frightened when

___ a. the election came.

___ b. he faced the student body.

___ c. he faced his family.

10. To be a good president, one must

___ a. be a good student.

___ b. listen to the administration.

___ c. maintain a working communication.

11. Mike was aware of

___ a. the presidency.

_____ b. his responsibilities.
_____ c. his election.

12. Mike pledged to

_____ a. strive to achieve common goals.
_____ b. become the president.
_____ c. have action.

13. Mike was sad and close to tears because

_____ a. his speech was better.
_____ b. his opponent's speech was good.
_____ c. the winner wasn't the best man.

14. Mike felt that the candidates were

_____ a. elected on popularity.
_____ b. elected fairly.
_____ c. better speakers than he.

B. Below there are three (3) different thoughts in each of the exercises. Assign the proper sequence (order) of **THOUGHT**, according to the narrative by numbering 1 to 3. Read aloud.

1. a. excited before   _____
   b. never been this   _____
   c. Mike has   _____

2. a. earlier than usual   _____
   b. home from school   _____
   c. he came   _____

3. a. in her son's behavior   _____
   b. Mrs. Campbell sensed   _____
   c. something unusual   _____

4. a. choice of candidates   _____
   b. they had a wide   _____
   c. I think   _____

5. a. get ahead of me   _____
   b. let my opponents   _____
   c. I can't   _____

6. a. I promise _____
   b. when it's all over _____
   c. I'll rest _____

7. a. all the time _____
   b. dress this way _____
   c. if only he would _____

8. a. Mike's dressing habits _____
   b. a complete change _____
   c. came over _____

9. a. in the past, _____
   b. seen in a tie at school _____
   c. he would never be _____

10. a. Mrs. Campbell _____
    b. to encourage Mike _____
    c. knew how _____

11. a. to prepare his speech _____
    b. easy for Mike _____
    c. it hadn't been _____

12. a. it should be said _____
    b. forcefully, Mike, the way _____
    c. you'll say it _____

13. a. to her son's words _____
    b. proudly listened _____
    c. Mrs. Campbell _____

14. a. the students and the administration _____
    b. a working communication between _____
    c. each president must dutifully maintain _____

15. a. if our requests are sensible _____
    b. response will be likewise sensible _____
    c. I'm sure that the _____

16. a. goals with the administration _____
    b. will strive to achieve common _____
    c. if I am elected I _____

17. a. any of theirs   _____
     b. better than   _____
     c. my speech was   _____

18. a. the vote is the voice   _____
     b. in our system   _____
     c. of the people   _____

19. a. to change that   _____
     b. some day   _____
     c. I'll work   _____

C.   There are some statements listed below about the narrative. Write **T** for **True** in front of each statement that you think is true. Write **F** for **False** if the statement is not true. Read aloud.

_____ 1. Mike was always excited.

_____ 2. He came home earlier than usual.

_____ 3. He spoke calmly to his mother.

_____ 4. Mrs. Campbell suggested a cola.

_____ 5. Mike told his mother he was president of the student body.

_____ 6. Mrs. Campbell cautioned her son.

_____ 7. Mike thought he had a good chance to win.

_____ 8. Mike went to sleep late.

_____ 9. He always ate supper with the family.

_____10. Mike was going to rest when he won.

_____11. Mike's dressing habits changed.

_____12. The Campbells listened to Mike's speech.

_____13. Mrs. Campbell didn't encourage her son.

_____14. It was easy for Mike to prepare his speech.

_____15. Mike said that there must be many requests.

_____16. He said that he was aware of his responsibilities.

_____17. He also said that he would strive to achieve common goals with the administration.

_____ 18. The following day Mike returned home happy.

_____ 19. The vote is the voice of the people.

_____ 20. Mike agreed with the way elections were held.

_____ 21. He promised to change the system.

X. *Composition and Discussion*

A. In COLUMN I are the beginnings of sentences. In COLUMN II are the completions to sentences of COLUMN I. Select the completion best fitting each sentence in COLUMN I according to the narrative. Read the completed sentences orally. Compose new sentences orally and discuss the narrative.

COLUMN I	COLUMN II
1. Mike has never been	a. as the Campbells had wished.
2. He came home from school	b. this way all the time.
3. They sat	c. on a merry-go-round.
4. I think they had	d. a good speech.
5. Mike was constantly	e. earlier than usual.
6. I would slow down	f. at the table.
7. I will rest	g. if I could.
8. If only he would dress	h. this excited before.
9. A complete change	i. for Mike to prepare his speech.
10. I'll impress people	j. tomorrow to listen.
11. I'll prepare	k. as a neat dresser.
12. Mrs. Campbell knew	l. when it's all over.
13. It hadn't been easy	m. how to encourage Mike.
14. I'll be at school	n. a wide choice of candidates.
15. We have a	o. came over Mike's dressing habits.
16. It was not	p. good school here.

B. 1. Tell us about an election.
    2. Tell us about Mike's speech.
    3. How did the Campbells help Mike?
    4. Why did Mike feel sad?
    5. Describe the change in Mike's behavior.

C.   Describe what you see in the picture below.

D.   Read the poem aloud. Answer orally the questions listed following the poem.

A Question

His life has gone with the winds of forgotten days.   [1] force
He will dream of none but the final truth.   [2] shake
He will seek a might[1] that trembles[2] not nor sways[3] [3] affect
That knows no aging transition[4] from youth . . .   [4] change

This force has no end such as this, for it had no beginning.
Can there be something greater? Tell me! Do!
Or is my very question condemned[5] for a sin?   [5] judged
Is there an idol more splendid[6] than truth?   [6] magnificent
                                                        [7] ridicule
Scorn[7] not the dying for asking reply[8]   [8] answer

To questions he has blindly accepted before.
He shall die seeking.[9] His work is done.
Soon he will find the answer at last . . .

[9] searching

1. Identify *present perfect* sentences.

2. Identify *future time* sentences.

3. Identify sentences containing *modal auxiliaries.*

4. Does the title express the idea of the entire poem?

5. In which stanza lies the expression of a *promise?*

* * * * * *

Chapter Six

The Enchanted Mountain

Words to remember:

Past Perfect Tense
had + past participle

Comparison = equal things
unequal things

very, too, so, + **Adjective (Adverb)**
and + too − and + so − but

I. *Narrative*

A.   Little Lucy was unable to explain why she had climbed the mountain to the very top. Had she been able to understand what had happened, she might have explained it to those who asked. As it was, as often as she tried, things got too involved. She decided instead to tell the entire story.

B.   That morning, it was very foggy, and Lucy lost her way completely. Before she knew how it had happened, she was at the foot of a huge green mountain. She had gone too far. There was no one there, but Lucy was not afraid. On the contrary, she became very curious and was too excited to think of danger. It seemed so easy to climb that Lucy looked forward to her ascent with great anticipation.

C.   When she had reached the very top, she was suddenly surrounded by a throng of small creatures. They were taller than herself, but they were shapeless and colorless. Many bathed in the clear water of the immense lake. She had never seen such creatures before. Nor had she been told they existed. It was too late for her to withdraw. Her presence was noticed, and she was afriad to move from the spot.

D.   Lucy was very frightened, and so were the little creatures. She remembered vaguely someone had told her that fear is caused by the unknown. Lucy smiled, and so did the faces of the little shapeless, colorless creatures. One of them, he seemed as frightened as the rest, stepped up closer to the girl.

E.   "Welcome to the Enchanted Mountain, Lucy," he said in perfect English, which surprised the little girl no end. "We are the Erutuf people," the creature continued, as though in response to Lucy's mute amazement. "We live on this mountain. Our ancestors have been its inhabitants before us." He paused for a moment. "You see the Erutuf bathing in the lake below? They're being punished for spreading gossip, for being greedy, and for being envious of other Erutuf people."

F.   "Is taking a bath punishment?" Lucy exclaimed. "It is, if you don't like taking a bath. We are known for that. We hate water!" the Erutuf cried louder than she had ever heard anyone cry. "Three baths daily are more than anyone can stand," he concluded seriously. Lucy was silent. She was too afraid to hurt the little creature's feelings.

G.   "But how could anyone be prejudiced in this place, among creatures without color and without shape?" Lucy asked without saying a word. Again, the little Erutuf caught her silent inquiry. "You'll be surprised to hear this, Lucy, but we do very simple things here. The simpler, the better. And what's simpler than hate and bigotry?" "Love!" Lucy replied quickly. "Do they love where you come from?" the Erutuf asked. Lucy didn't know how to answer that. She kept silent.

H.   "We found a way to punish the incorrigibles more severely than the mere repeaters. They are given color and shape. Then, they are banished from the top to the mountainside. From there, they must work their way up to the top for thirteen years. When they become colorless and shapeless again, they are accepted in our community. And all the time refuse is their food. We push that over the side too. There's nothing else they can eat."

I. "I wish to leave this place right now!" Lucy cried. "I want to go home to my family. Please, let me go! You are more cruel than anyone I know. Even Miss Conklin, the history teacher!" At the first sight of tears, even quicker than you could say "Erutuf," the little creatures were all gone. The bathers were gone too. Only Lucy was left, her eyes closed, alone and no longer frightened.

J. When she opened her eyes, she was with her family. There was a look of concern in her parents' faces. Lucy sensed that something had happened. She knew that she would have to explain. Grown-ups always want things explained. But as hard as she tried, Lucy was unable to explain. She decided then it would be better to draw them a picture. Someday, she would do this, not just now.

* * *

II. Words in Context [*Pictographs*]

Below are some of the words used in the narrative. Where possible, each word has a [synonym], or it is defined as used in the story. Where possible, an [antonym] is also given. Make up sentences about the pictographs choosing the words you need. Read aloud.

Example: [ascend] = She ascended the mountain.

A. and B.

explain [tell clearly] (*obscure*); climb [ascend] (*descend*); mountain [large hill] (*valley*); top [summit] (*bottom*); involved [confused, intricate] (*simple*); decide [determine] (*doubt*); instead [in place of] ; foggy [misty] (*clear*); completely [entirely] (*not at all*); huge [enormous] (*diminutive*); contrary [opposite] ; curious [inquiring] (*indifferent*); danger [peril] (*safety*); forward [ahead] (*backward*); anticipation [expectation] (*misapprehension*)

C. and D.

reach [arrive at] (*revert*); suddenly [abruptly] (*gradually*); surround [encircle] ; throng [crowd] ; creature [being] ; tall [high] (*short*); shapeless [formless] (*formed*); colorless [lacking hue] (*colorful*); clear [transparent] (*muddy*); immense [enormous] (*tiny*); exist [live] (*die*); move

Drawing of paragraph A & B

[stir] (*rest*); spot [place] ; vaguely [indefinitely] (*definitely*); unknown [unfamiliar] (*known*)

E. F. and G.

enchanted [charmed] (*disenchanted*); perfect [faultless] (*imperfect*); amazed [surprised] (*unamazed*); ancestor [forebear] (*descendant*); inhabitant [occupant] ; punish [chastise] (*reward*); spread [circulate] ; gossip [spread rumor] (*be discrete*); greedy [avaricious] (*generous*); envious [jealous] (*satisfied*); hate [detest] (*love*); loud [noisy] (quiet); stand [tolerate] ; prejudice [bigotry] (*fairness*); inquiry [question] (*statement*); surprise [astonish] (*forewarn*); simple [uncomplicated] (*complicated*)

H. I. and J.

incorrigible [hopeless] (*hopeful*); severely [harshly] (*leniently*); banish [exile] (*shelter*); side [edge] (*center*); work [labor] (*rest*); community

Drawing of paragraph C & D

[society] (*disunity*); refuse [garbage] ; cruel [inhuman] (*humane*); sight [seeing] (*blindness*); try [attempt] (*abandon*)

III. Structures *[Phrases]*

Below are some PHRASES taken from the narrative. Make complete sentences and read them aloud.

A.	unable	—	to	—	explain
B.	to	—	the	—	very top
C.	able	—	to	—	understand
D.	those	—	who	—	asked
E.	as	—	she	—	tried
F.	of	—	that	—	day
G.	how	—	it	—	had happened

Drawing of paragraph E, F & G

H.	at	—	the	—	foot
I.	so	—	easy	—	to climb
J.	reached	—	the	—	very top
K.	they	—	were	—	shapeless
L.	in	—	the	—	clear water
M.	late	—	for her	—	to withdraw
N.	move	—	from	—	the spot
O.	caused	—	by	—	the unknown
P.	closer	—	to	—	the girl
Q.	in	—	answer	—	to
R.	in	—	the lake	—	below
S.	for	—	spreading	—	gossip
T.	if	—	you	—	don't like
U.	more	—	than	—	anyone
V.	too	—	afraid	—	to hurt
W.	prejudiced	—	in	—	this place
X.	the	—	simple	—	things

Drawing of paragraph H, I and J

Y.	from	–	the	–	top
Z.	up	–	to the	–	top

IV. *Sentences*

A. Read the following sentences aloud. Repeat, substituting where possible, the synonym of the word in *italics,* or a phrase that explains the meaning. Make other necessary changes.

   Example: Lucy could not *clear up* the story.
   Lucy was unable to *explain* the story.

1. She had seen a *huge* mountain.
2. They are *banished* from the top.
3. They must *work* their way up.
4. They had been *punished.*

5. *Refuse* is their food.
6. We had pushed that over the *side.*
7. There's nothing else the *community* can do.
8. I had *tried* to leave this place.
9. You are full of *prejudice.*
10. The little *creatures* were gone.
11. The bathers were very *loud.*
12. Only Lucy was *enchanted.*
13. She was no longer *involved.*
14. She *determined to* open her eyes.
15. She was out of *peril.*
16. There was a look of *concern.*
17. Lucy *sensed* that something had happened.
18. She had to explain the *unfamiliar* place.
19. Lucy was *unable* to do it.
20. She had been *astonished.*

B.   Fill in the blanks with words from the narrative. Each space may be filled
by a word or phrase. Do not refer back to the narrative. Where possible,
use variations of the missing words. Read aloud.

Little Lucy was unable to _____ why she _____ the mountain to
the very_____ . _____ she _____ able to _____what happened, she might
_____ explained it to _____ who _____ .

On the_____of that day, it was _____ and Lucy lost her_____
completely. She was at the _____of a _____ green _____ . It_____ so
easy to _____ that Lucy looked _____to her _____ with great _____ .

When she _____ the very top, she _____ suddenly _____ by a
_____ of small creatures. They were_____ than _____ , but they were
_____ and _____ . She _____ never _____ such creatures.

Lucy was _____ , and so _____ the little _____ . She _____ vaguely
someone _____ her that fear is _____ by the_____ . Lucy_____ ,
and so did the _____ of the_____ shapeless, _____ creatures. One of
_____ stepped up _____to the girl.

"Welcome to the _____ , Lucy," he said in _____ English. "We are
the Erutuf_____ ," the _____ continued. "We live on this_____ . Our
_____ been its inhabitants _____ us." He _____ for a moment.
"The Erutuf bathing in the _____ are being _____ for _____ gossip."

"Is taking a _____ punishment?" Lucy_____ amazed. "It is, if you
don't _____taking a _____ . We are _____ for that. We _____water!" The
Erutuf_____louder _____ she _____ ever _____ anyone cry. "Three
_____ daily are _____ than anyone can _____ ."

"But how could anyone be_____ in this place, _____ creatures without

_____ and without _____?" Lucy _____ without saying a _____ . "You'll
be _____ to hear this, Lucy, but we _____ very _____ things here. The
_____ , the _____ . And what's _____ than _____ and _____ ?" "Love!"
Lucy _____ quickly.

"We found a _____ to _____ the _____ more _____ than the mere
_____ . They are given _____ and _____ . Then, they are _____ from the
_____ to the _____ . From there, they must _____ their way _____ to the
_____ for thirteen _____ . When they _____ colorless and _____ again,
they are _____ in our community.

"I wish to _____ this _____ right now!" Lucy cried. "I want to go _____
to my _____!" At the _____ sight of _____ , even _____ than you could
say "Erutuf, the _____ creatures were all _____ . The _____ were _____
too.

When Lucy _____ her eyes, she was _____ her _____ . She _____ that
something _____ happened. She knew that she _____ have to _____ .
Grown-ups _____ want _____ explained.

V.   *Grammar and Syntax   (Points of Interest)*

A.   The **Past Perfect** refers to an *event* that happened before *another event* in
the past. The *other* event is usually introduced by *when* or an expression
that answers *when.* The past perfect also occurs in *dependent clauses.* The
verb in the *main clause* is in the *past tense.* Sometimes the reverse is true.

Little Lucy *was unable* to explain why she *had climbed* the mountain.

She might *have explained* it, *had* she *been able* to understand.

She *was* suddenly *surrounded* when she *had reached* the top.

- -

B.   **Comparison** means to compare two *equal* things (*as. . .as*), or to compare
two *unequal* things (*-er than* or *more than*).

1. Two *equal* things:

As often *as* she tried, things got too involved.

One of them seemed *as* much frightened *as* the rest.

They're being punished for spreading gossip *as* well *as* for being envious.

As hard *as* she tried, Lucy was unable to explain.

2. Two *unequal* things:

The Erutuf cried *louder than* she had ever heard anyone cry.

They were *taller than* Lucy.

What's *simpler than* hate and bigotry?

Punish them *more severely than* repeaters.

Even *quicker than* you could say "Erutuf."

It would be *better* to draw them a picture.

— — — — — — — — — — — — — — — — — — — —

C.   1. Use of the words *very, too, so + Adjective (Adverb):*

Lucy became *very curious.*
It was *very foggy* and she lost her way.
Lucy was *very frightened.*
We do the *very simple* things here.

She had gone *too far.*
It was *too late* for her to withdraw.
She was *too afraid* to hurt his feelings.

It was *so foggy* that she lost her way.
It seemed *so easy* to climb that Lucy looked forward to it.

2. Use of *and + too:*

We are small, *and* you *are too.*
Lucy was frightened *and* they *were too.*
We are punished, *and* they *are too.*
The Erutuf cried, *and* Lucy *did too.*

3. Use of *and + so:*

Lucy was frightened, *and so were* the little creatures.
Lucy smiled, *and so did* the faces of the creatures.
One of them stepped up closer, *and so did* the others.
They're being punished, *and so are* the others.

4. Use of *but:*

Lucy wanted to explain, *but* she did not understand.

There was no one there, *but* Lucy was not afraid.
They were taller, *but* they were shapeless.
You'll be surprised, *but* we do simple things here.

VI.   *Word Recognition*

A.   Circle the word in Column II most *like* the word in Column I, and the word in Column III most *unlike* the word in Column I. This oral identification of words ought to be timed.

	COLUMN I		COLUMN II		COLUMN III
1.	completely	a.	entirely	a.	favorable
		b.	contrary	b.	diminutive
		c.	adverse	c.	not at all
2.	cruel	a.	nice	a.	gentle
		b.	healthy	b.	humane
		c.	inhuman	c.	loving
3.	danger	a.	curiosity	a.	decision
		b.	peril	b.	security
		c.	inquiry	c.	misapprehension
4.	explain	a.	clear up	a.	decide
		b.	involve	b.	determine
		c.	implicate	c.	obscure
5.	foggy	a.	entire	a.	contrary
		b.	whole	b.	clear
		c.	misty	c.	opposite
6.	greedy	a.	avaricious	a.	loud
		b.	unfamiliar	b.	familiar
		c.	jealous	c.	generous
7.	immense	a.	curious	a.	tiny
		b.	enormous	b.	tall
		c.	crowded	c.	high
8.	incorrigible	a.	complex	a.	generous
		b.	greedy	b.	hopeful
		c.	hopeless	c.	satisfied

9. **inquiry**
    a. bias
    b. question
    c. prejudice

    a. statement
    b. fairness
    c. love

10. **mountain**
    a. top
    b. large hill
    c. summit

    a. valley
    b. bottom
    c. forest

11. **open**
    a. candid
    b. free
    c. contrary

    a. simple
    b. secretive
    c. senseless

12. **perfect**
    a. commonplace
    b. faultless
    c. charmed

    a. disenchanted
    b. complex
    c. imperfect

13. **punish**
    a. gossip
    b. spread rumor
    c. chastise

    a. reward
    b. be discrete
    c. circulate

14. **reach**
    a. move
    b. stir
    c. arrive at

    a. revert
    b. rest
    c. clear

15. **severely**
    a. loudly
    b. noisily
    c. harshly

    a. leniently
    b. quietly
    c. slowly

16. **shapeless**
    a. colorless
    b. formless
    c. lacking hue

    a. formed
    b. translucent
    c. clear

17. **side**
    a. mountain
    b. edge
    c. top

    a. center
    b. valley
    c. bottom

18. **suddenly**
    a. severely
    b. slowly
    c. abruptly

    a. gradually
    b. ably
    c. gently

19. **surprise**
    a. try
    b. astonish
    c. love

    a. forewarn
    b. slow down
    c. explain

20. **vaguely**   a.   temporarily   a.   definitely
                         b.   anonymously   b.   knowingly
                         c.   indefinitely   c.   lively

B.   In the space on the left write the word(s) that best fit the expression in **bold print**. Make other necessary changes. Read aloud.

_____   1. Lucy was unable to **tell clearly** why she climbed the mountain.

_____   2. She **determined** to tell the story.

_____   3. It was very **foggy**.

_____   4. She lost her way **entirely**.

_____   5. Lucy was at the foot of a **huge** mountain.

_____   6. She was too curious to think of **peril**.

_____   7. She was **suddenly surrounded**.

_____   8. There was a **crowd** of small creatures.

_____   9. They were **formless**.

_____   10. There was an **enormous** lake.

_____   11. Lucy could not move from the **spot**.

_____   12. This is the **charmed** mountain.

_____   13. He spoke English to Lucy's **astonishment**.

_____   14. Those in the lake were being **chastised**.

_____   15. They were punished for being **avaricious**.

_____   16. We **detest** water.

_____   17. How could anyone be **biased** here?

_____   18. You'll be **astonished** to hear this.

_____   19. We do very **uncomplicated** things here.

_____   20. She replied **promptly**.

_____   21. We found a way to punish the **hopeless**.

_____   22. They are punished more **severely**.

_____   23. They are **exiled** from the top.

VII. *Concept Recognition*

Fill in the most appropriate word (phrase) to express the CONCEPT of the sentence according to the narrative. Read the complete sentence aloud.

A. Little Lucy climbed to the top of the mountain, but she was unable to _____ it.

1. explain	2. separate
3. involve	4. implicate

B. She could not explain, because she was not able to _____ it herself.

1. decide	2. determine
3. understand	4. wave

C. Because it was foggy, Lucy had _____ her way.

1. cleared	2. lost
3. reached	4. grasped

D. Lucy was not _____ , even though no one was there.

1. colorless	2. curious
3. lacking hue	4. afraid

E. Her excitement made her forget the _____ .

1. danger	2. forestallment
3. anticipation	4. misapprehension

F. She looked forward to her ascent because it _____ .

1. seemed easy	2. was contrary
3. was dangerous	4. was ahead

G. The creatures were small, but they were _____ than Lucy.

1. clearer	2. taller
3. more shapeless	4. colorless

H. She had never seen such creatures. She didn't know they _____ .

1. existed	2. encircled
3. surrounded	4. missed

I. It was too late for her to withdraw because her _____ was _____ .

1. throng, translucent   2. danger, known
3. presence, noticed   4. smile, unknown

J.   Lucy was very_____ , and so were the little creatures.

   1. immense   2. definite
   3. frightened   4. clear

K.   Because someone had told her, she knew that _____ was caused by the _____ .

   1. fear, unknown   2. throng, creatures
   3. spot, known   4. crowd, beings

L.   When Lucy_____ , the faces of the Erutuf _____ also.

   1. talked, talked   2. smiled, smiled
   3. reached, reached   4. moved, moved

M.   Even though Lucy did not_____ , the Erutuf knew what she wanted to say.

   1. speak   2. reach
   3. move   4. liberate

N.   The Erutuf people lived on the mountain because their _____ lived there before them.

   1. unknown   2. throng
   3. anonymous   4. ancestors

O.   Those Erutuf who bathed in the lake were being _____ .

   1. rewarded   2. chastised
   3. loved   4. hated

P.   Lucy was silent because she didn't want to _____ the little creature.

   1. investigate   2. conjecture
   3. hurt   4. love

Q.   Lucy didn't understand how anyone could be_____ on the mountain.

   1. prejudiced   2. hated
   3. loved   4. astonished

R.   Lucy wanted to return home because she thought that the Erutuf were
_____ .

     1. prejudiced   2. cruel
     3. biased   4. quiet

S.   Lucy knew she would have to _____ because grown-ups want things
_____ .

     1. explain, explained   2. hate, loved
     3. stand, simple   4. punish, rewarded

VIII.   *Telling the Meaning*

A.   Place a check mark (✓) in front of the word in COLUMN II that best fits
the MEANING of the word in COLUMN I. Read aloud a complete
sentence using this word.

     COLUMN I   COLUMN II

1. **abruptly**
         _____ a.   gradually
         _____ b.   completely
         _____ c.   suddenly

2. **arrive at**
         _____ a.   reach
         _____ b.   anticipate
         _____ c.   revert

3. **avaricious**
         _____ a.   unfamiliar
         _____ b.   greedy
         _____ c.   generous

4. **chastise**
         _____ a.   reward
         _____ b.   punish
         _____ c.   forewarn

5. **climb**
         _____ a.   descend
         _____ b.   ascend
         _____ c.   walk

6. **colorless**
         _____ a.   lacking hue
         _____ b.   clear
         _____ c.   colorful

7. **community**   _____ a.   society
                          _____ b.   feeling
                          _____ c.   segregation

8. **completely**   _____ a.   not at all
                          _____ b.   entirely
                          _____ c.   contrary

9. **curious**   _____ a.   adverse
                          _____ b.   indifferent
                          _____ c.   inquiring

10. **danger**   _____ a.   peril
                          _____ b.   question
                          _____ c.   security

11. **decide**   _____ a.   doubt
                          _____ b.   determine
                          _____ c.   part

12. **enormous**   _____ a.   tiny
                          _____ b.   immense
                          _____ c.   curious

13. **exist**   _____ a.   die
                          _____ b.   live
                          _____ c.   move

14. **faultless**   _____ a.   imperfect
                          _____ b.   perfect
                          _____ c.   charmed

15. **formless**   _____ a.   formed
                          _____ b.   high
                          _____ c.   shapeless

16. **forward**   _____ a.   contrary
                          _____ b.   backward
                          _____ c.   ahead

17. **gossip**   _____ a.   be discrete
                          _____ b.   spread rumor
                          _____ c.   be jealous

18. **hopeless**
     _____ a.   hopeful
     _____ b.   humane
     _____ c.   incorrigible

19. **large hill**
     _____ a.   top
     _____ b.   valley
     _____ c.   mountain

20. **misty**
     _____ a.   foggy
     _____ b.   whole
     _____ c.   clear

21. **prejudice**
     _____ a.   fairness
     _____ b.   hate
     _____ c.   bigotry

22. **question**
     _____ a.   warning
     _____ b.   inquiry
     _____ c.   conjecture

23. **simple**
     _____ a.   complicated
     _____ b.   complete
     _____ c.   uncomplicated

24. **smile**
     _____ a.   spot
     _____ b.   grin
     _____ c.   frown

25. **surround**
     _____ a.   encircle
     _____ b.   crowd
     _____ c.   liberate

26. **unknown**
     _____ a.   vague
     _____ b.   unfamiliar
     _____ c.   known

B.   Return to Exercise A. Place two check marks (✓✓) in front of the word in COLUMN II that is the ANTONYM of the word in COLUMN I. Read aloud a complete sentence using this word.

C.   Select one of the three (3) words (phrases) that best fulfills the MEANING of the sentence according to the narrative. Insert the word in the blank space. Read the completed sentence aloud.

1. Lucy was unable to explain why she had climbed the mountain because she did not_____it herself.
   a. understand   b. clear up   c. obscure

2. She tried many times to explain, but things got too_____.
   a. obscure   b. involved   c. separated

3. Lucy was not afraid because she became very_____.
   a. clear   b. excited   c. adverse

4. She looked forward to her ascent because it seemed_____to climb.
   a. clear   b. contrary   c. easy

5. Lucy thought there was no one, but she was_____by a throng of creatures.
   a. liberated   b. surrounded   c. formed

6. She wanted to withdraw, but she didn't_____because her presence was noticed.
   a. stir   b. exist   c. die

7. She remembered that fear is caused by the_____and she smiled.
   a. known   b. definite   c. unknown

8. Though Lucy didn't say a word, the little creatures_____her questions.
   a. answered   b. declared   c. punished

9. The Erutuf people bathed in the lake because they were being_____.
   a. chastised   b. rewarded   c. hated

10. Lucy was silent because she didn't want to_____the creature's feelings.
    a. love   b. hurt   c. prejudice

11. Though the Erutuf were colorless and shapeless, they were_____.
    a. kind   b. bigoted   c. fair

12. There was a way to punish the_____by giving them color and shape.
    a. occupants   b. people   c. incorrigibles

13. Because they were being punished, the incorrigibles received_____for food.
    a. fairness   b. love   c. refuse

14. Lucy knew she would have to explain because grown-ups
_____ explained.
  a. refuse slow   b. see work   c. want things

IX. Comprehension [Exercises]

A.   Place a check mark (✓) in front of the correct response to each of the statements according to the narrative. Read the complete sentence aloud.

1. Lucy was unable to explain why she had climbed the mountain because

   _____ a. she was afraid.
   _____ b. she didn't understand it herself.
   _____ c. she didn't want to.

2. She decided

   _____ a. to tell the whole story.
   _____ b. to get things involved.
   _____ c. to try.

3. Because it was very foggy, Lucy
   _____ a. climbed the mountain.
   _____ b. lost her way.
   _____ c. was afraid.

4. The mountain was

   _____ a. small and dark.
   _____ b. like a hill.
   _____ c. huge and green.

5. Lucy became curious and too excited

   _____ a. to climb the mountain.
   _____ b. to think of danger.
   _____ c. to go too far.

6. She looked forward to her ascent because

   _____ a. it seemed easy to climb.
   _____ b. it seemed difficult to climb.
   _____ c. it was clear.

7. When Lucy reached the top

_____ a. she was alone.
_____ b. she was at home.
_____ c. she was surrounded by creatures.

8. The small creatures were

_____ a. clear and known.
_____ b. shapeless and colorless.
_____ c. Lucy's friends.

9. Lucy did not withdraw because

_____ a. she was tired.
_____ b. her presence was noticed.
_____ c. she liked the creatures.

10. When Lucy smiled,

_____ a. no one spoke to her.
_____ b. she was frightened.
_____ c. so did the faces of the little creatures.

11. The little creature

_____ a. welcomed Lucy.
_____ b. was surprised.
_____ c. was unfriendly.

12. The Erutuf people were punished for

_____ a. crying loudly.
_____ b. being greedy and envious.
_____ c. being kind.

13. The Erutuf people were punished

_____ a. by hating water.
_____ b. by loving water.
_____ c. by taking a bath.

14. The incorrigibles were punished when

_____ a. they talked with Lucy.
_____ b. they took a bath.
_____ c. they were given food.

15. The incorrigibles could return to their community when

_____ a. they loved one another.
_____ b. they became colorless and shapeless.
_____ c. they ate refuse.

16. Because Lucy was unable to explain, she decided
_____ a. to draw a picture.
_____ b. to climb the mountain.
_____ c. to take her parents to the mountain.

B. Below there are three (3) different thoughts in each of the exercises. Assign the proper sequence (order) of THOUGHT, according to the narrative, by numbering 1 to 3. Read aloud.

1. a. the mountain to the very top _____
   b. why she had climbed _____
   c. little Lucy was unable to explain _____

2. a. the entire story _____
   b. to tell _____
   c. she decided instead _____

3. a. on the morning of that day _____
   b. it was very foggy and Lucy _____
   c. lost her way completely _____

4. a. was not afraid _____
   b. there, but Lucy _____
   c. there was no one _____

5. a. it seemed so easy to climb, _____
   b. ascent with great anticipation _____
   c. that Lucy looked forward to her _____

6. a. shapeless and colorless _____
   b. they were taller than _____
   c. herself, but they were _____

7. a. many bathed _____
   b. of the immense lake _____
   c. in the clear water _____

8. a. to move from the spot ————————
   b. her presence was noticed, ————————
   c. and she was afraid ————————

9. a. the little creatures ————————
   b. and so were ————————
   c. Lucy was very frightened, ————————

10. a. someone had told her ————————
    b. she remembered vaguely ————————
    c. that fear is caused by the unknown ————————

11. a. the creature continued, ————————
    b. "We are the Erutuf people." ————————
    c. as though in response to Lucy's mute amazement ————————

12. a. before us ————————
    b. had been its inhabitants ————————
    c. our ancestors ————————

13. a. Lucy exclaimed, ————————
    b. a bath punishment?" ————————
    c. "is taking ————————

14. a. heard anyone cry ————————
    b. than she had ever ————————
    c. the Erutuf cried louder ————————

15. a. anyone can stand ————————
    b. daily are more than ————————
    c. three baths ————————

16. a. the little creature's feelings ————————
    b. afraid to hurt ————————
    c. she was too ————————

17. a. very simple things here ————————
    b. hear this, Lucy, but we do ————————
    c. you'll be surprised to ————————

18. a. we found a way to punish ————————
    b. the incorrigibles more severely ————————
    c. than the mere repeaters ————————

19. a. they are accepted in our community _____
    b. when they become _____
    c. colorless and shapeless again _____

20. a. that over _____
    b. we push _____
    c. the side too _____

21. a. alone and no longer frightened _____
    b. her eyes closed, _____
    c. only Lucy was left, _____

22. a. she was _____
    b. when she had opened her eyes _____
    c. among her family _____

23. a. to draw them a picture _____
    b. it would be better _____
    c. she decided then _____

C. There are some statements listed below about the narrative. Write **T** for **True** in front of each statement that you think is true. Write **F** for **False** if the statement is not true. Read aloud.

_____ 1. Lucy didn't want to explain.

_____ 2. She was able to understand.

_____ 3. Lucy decided to tell the story.

_____ 4. It was foggy when she climbed the mountain.

_____ 5. Lucy thought of the danger.

_____ 6. She looked forward to her ascent.

_____ 7. At the top she was suddenly surrounded.

_____ 8. The small creatures were smaller than Lucy.

_____ 9. She had been told they existed.

_____ 10. It was too late for her to withdraw.

_____ 11. Lucy was not frightened, but the creatures were.

_____ 12. She smiled and so did the creatures.

_____ 13. The creatures were shapeless and colorless.

_____ 14. One of the creatures spoke to Lucy.

_____ 15. The creature did not speak English.

_____ 16. There were Erutuf people bathing in the lake.

_____ 17. The Erutuf people liked taking a bath.

_____ 18. The bathers were being punished.

_____ 19. They were punished for greed.

_____ 20. Lucy was afraid to hurt the little creature's feelings.

_____ 21. The Erutuf people do simple things.

_____ 22. The incorrigibles were punished more severely than mere repeaters.

_____ 23. The incorrigibles became colorless and shapeless.

_____ 24. The incorrigibles were given good food.

_____ 25. When Lucy cried, the Erutuf people disappeared.

_____ 26. Lucy decided to explain things to her parents.

X.   *Composition and Discussion*

A.   In COLUMN I are the beginnings of sentences. In COLUMN II are the
completions to sentences of COLUMN I. Select the completion best fitting
each sentence in COLUMN I according to the narrative. Read the
completed sentences orally. Compose new sentences orally and discuss the
narrative.

COLUMN I	COLUMN II
1. Lucy was unable to explain	a. the top of the mountain.
2. As often as she tried	b. she was with her family.
3. There was no one there, ...	c. in the clear water.
4. She became very curious	d. in her parents' faces.
5. Lucy looked forward to her	e. color and shape.
6. She was suddenly surrounded . . .	f. but Lucy was not afraid.
7. They were taller, ...	g. and too excited to think of danger.
8. Many bathed	h. but they were shapeless.
9. She had never seen	i. ascent with anticipation.
10. It was too late	j. things got too involved.

11. Someone had told her ....   k. why she had climbed the mountain.

12. Our ancestors had been ....   l. such creatures before.

13. The Erutuf cried louder ....   m. for her to withdraw.

14. Three baths daily are more ......   n. than she had heard anyone cry.

15. The simpler ....   o. they can eat.

16. Do they love ....   p. this place right now!

17. The incorrigibles are given ......   q. better to draw a picture.

18. They are banished from ....   r. where you come from?

19. There's nothing else ....   s. she would have to explain.

20. I wish to leave ....   t. Lucy was unable to explain.

21. When she opened her eyes ......   u. by a throng of small creatures.

22. There was a look of concern ....   v. that fear is caused by the unknown.

23. She knew that ....   w. its inhabitants before us.

24. As hard as she tried, ...   x. the better.

25. She decided it would be ....   y. than anyone can stand.

B.   1. Tell us about climbing a mountain.

       2. Describe the small creatures.

       3. Why was Lucy frightened?

       4. How did the Erutuf people punish greed and prejudice?

       5. What do you think of the Erutuf society?

C.   Read the poem aloud. Answer orally the questions listed following the poem.

To Be Different

Why is it that so many who
had wished to be different,
have become so like
one another?

They defy[1] individuality which   [1] go against
they had seemingly pursued.[2]   [2] striven for
They dress alike, one face
shows less originality than another.

And so in speech and thought
they are but images[3]   [3] mirrors

of each other. The
songs they rhythmically

produce pulsate mediocrity
no better than the very
ways of imitation they despise![4]   [4] hate
And there seems no end to that. . .

1. What do the words "different" and "individuality" have in common? Discuss in class.
2. Read aloud the lines containing *"so."* Discuss meaning.
3. Read aloud the lines containing *"but."* Discuss meaning.
4. Read aloud sentences with the *past perfect.*
5. Tell about the meaning of this poem.

D.   Describe what you see in the picture below.

* * * * * *

Chapter Seven

The Cave

Words to remember:

The passive voice
The active voice
The imperative mood — *Let's + infinitive*

I. *Narrative*

A. When summer came, the Campbells were thinking about vacation. The children looked forward to the annual family trip. Everybody did except Mike, for he was planning a vacation of his own. His cousin Weldon was coming from Wisconsin for the summer. Mike became interested in spelunking when he heard that Weldon had explored caves for over a year. "Don't you forget it," Mrs. Campbell warned Mike. "You must be careful exploring caves." "I'm not a child, Mother." Mike acted hurt. "Even adults get into trouble when they get careless down there," Mrs. Campbell

153

hastened to add. "What mother's saying, is that she cares what happens to you. Do take precautions," Mr. Campbell said. "Sure we will! After all, Weldon is an experienced spelunker," Mike assured his parents.

B.   Weldon arrived on Saturday, as planned. Immediately, the two cousins began their preparations. "Bring a sleeping bag," Weldon reminded Mike, "like the one I have." He showed his sleeping bag to Mike. "It gets very cold in the hills," Weldon added with a smile. "And don't ever leave your lamp behind," he concluded.

C.   The sheriff's deputy in New Braunfels wrote down their names. He also asked the boys to stay at the indicated location. It was assumed that small undiscovered caves could be found in the hills near New Braunfels. "If you haven't shown up in three days, the boys'll come up to get you," the sheriff said with a broad grin. "You shouldn't be there alone very long," the deputy said. "Go down slowly, and be careful, boys," he cautioned as they shook hands saying goodbye.

D.   Below a large limestone bridge, the two explorers saw a hole. They dug further. A cave was suddenly discovered by Mike. The boys felt a draft of cool air coming through the rock and debris. As they descended, they were hit by small falling rocks. "Let's get down lower, Mike! Please hand me the lamp!" Weldon was excited.

E.   Further digging revealed a twisting, downward passage which opened into a cave. The two explorers crawled through a vast labyrinth of columns and crystalline formations. "Mike, hand me the rope," Weldon demanded. "To get down, you must use the rope," he added, getting ready to descend.

F.   Suddenly, Weldon lost his footing. The lamp fell downward. As it hit against the walls, the noise multiplied throughout with an echo. Finally, the lamp hit bottom deep below. Weldon did not fall very far. His voice came clearly from below as Mike listened anxiously. "My foot is wedged in between two rocks. The place is too narrow to free it. I think my left ankle is fractured. The pain is terrific." It was dark without the lamp, but Weldon felt his way around. "There's a large skeleton down here. It feels like a large animal, maybe a grizzly," he called to Mike. "Do be careful down there!" Mike yelled. "I'll go get help!" "Don't worry, Mike. The grizzly's probably been dead for more than eight thousand years." "Don't joke. I'll be back soon."

G.   Mike returned half an hour later accompanied by two sheriff's deputies. He was lucky the officers were already searching the hills for them as they'd promised. Weldon was glad to hear voices above. "I almost gave up on you," he called when he heard the voices of his rescuers. Soon, one of the deputies was lowered on a rope ladder. "Always descend carefully," the deputy cautioned. "It was an accident," Mike said. "It could happen to anybody."

H.   Everything went fine. A rope was tied round Weldon's waist. The deputy above, with Mike's help, pulled Weldon carefully upward. Below, the deputy spread the rocks with a crowbar, releasing Weldon's ankle. Mike descended to help. Soon, everybody emerged on the surface. The deputy examined the injury carefully. "Say, it's not a fracture after all. At the most, it's a sprained ankle." Everyone was relieved to be safe.

* * *

II.   *Words in Context*   *[Pictographs]*

Below are some of the words used in the narrative. Where possible, each word has a [synonym], or it is defined as used in the story. Where possible, an (*antonym*) is also given. Make up sentences about the pictographs choosing the words you need. Read aloud.

Example: [**spelunking**] = Mike was interested in spelunking.

A. and B.

Drawing of paragraph A and B

look forward to **[anticipate]** (*dread*); annual **[yearly]**; spelunking **[cave exploring]**; explore **[investigate]** (*ignore*); cave **[underground chamber]**; warn **[caution]** (*encourage*); trouble **[difficulty]** (*pleasure*); careless **[reckless]** (*careful*); hasten **[hurry]** (*slow down*); precaution **[care]** (*carelessness*); assure **[promise]**; immediately **[at once]** (*later*); preparation **[arrangement]** (*unpreparedness*)

C., D. and E.

Drawing of paragraph C, D, and E

sheriff **[county law enforcement officer]**; deputy **[representative of law enforcement]**; indicated **[specified]** (*unspecified*); location **[place]**; assume **[suppose]** (*know*); discover **[find]** (*search*); broad **[wide]** (*narrow*); bridge **[span]**; hole **[opening]**; dig **[excavate]** (*bury*); draft **[current]**; rock **[large stone]**; debris **[rubble]**; reveal **[disclose]** (*hide*); twisting **[curving]** (*straight*); crawl **[creep]** (*run*); vast **[immense]** (*small*); labyrinth **[maze]** (*straight passage*); crystalline **[clear]** (*unclear*); rope **[cord]**; footing **[support]**; multiply **[increase]** (*decrease*); echo **[reverberation]**; halt **[end]** (*continue*); deep **[buried]** (*shallow*); clearly

F., G. and H.

Drawing of paragraph F, G, and H

[plainly] (*indistinctly*); wedge [constrict] (*release*); narrow [tight] (*wide*); fracture [break] (*mend*); dark [obscure] (*light*); skeleton [bony framework]; joke [josh] (*be serious*); accompany [escort] (*be alone*); lucky [fortunate] (*unfortunate*); search [look for] (*discover*); rescue [save] (*endanger*); lower [let down] (*raise*); accident [mishap] (*plan*); tie [secure] (*untie*); pull [tow] (*push*); spread [separate] (*converge*); release [free] (*confine*); emerge [come out] (*go in*); examine [investigate] (*answer*); injury [damage]; sprained [twisted]

III. Structures [Phrases]

Below are some *phrases* taken from the narrative. Make complete sentences and read them aloud.

A.	about	—	vacation		
B.	forward	—	to	—	trip
C.	everybody	—	except	—	Mike
D.	of	—	his	—	own
E.	for	—	the	—	summer
F.	interested	—	in	—	spelunking
G.	for	—	over	—	a year
H.	when	—	careless		
I.	that	—	she	—	cares
J.	an	—	experienced	—	spelunker
K.	on Saturday	—	as	—	planned
L.	to	—	stay	—	at
M.	at	—	the	—	location
N.	to	—	be	—	found
O.	in	—	the	—	hills
P.	in	—	three	—	days
Q.	with	—	a broad	—	grin
R.	as	—	they	—	shook hands
S.	below	—	a	—	bridge
T.	of	—	cool	—	air
U.	through	—	the	—	rock
V.	against	—	the	—	walls
W.	somewhere	—	deep	—	below
X.	like	—	a large	—	animal
Y.	already	—	searching		
Z.	round	—	Weldon's	—	waist

IV. Sentences

A. Read the following sentences aloud. Repeat, substituting where possible, the synonym of the word in *italics,* or a phrase that explains the meaning. Make other necessary changes.

Example: Mike *promised* to be careful.
   Mike *assured* his mother he would be careful.

1. The children *looked forward* to the trip.
2. You must be careful *exploring caves.*
3. Weldon *warned*.
4. Mike *assured* his parents.
5. Weldon *arrived* on Saturday.
6. They began their *preparations.*
7. The *sheriff* took down their names.

8. Small *caves* could be found in the hills.
9. A cave was *discovered.*
10. They were hit by small *rocks.*
11. They crawled through a *labyrinth.*
12. The foot was *wedged* in between rocks.
13. He saw *clearly* a skeleton down there.
14. It was a *narrow* passage.
15. Weldon *crawled* into the cave.
16. The deputy examined the *fracture.*

B. Fill in the following blanks with words from the narrative. Each space may be filled by a word or phrase. Do not refer back to the narrative. Where possible, use variations of the missing words. Read aloud.

When summer_____, the Campbells _____ about vacation. The children looked_____ to the annual_____ trip. Mike was_____ a vacation of his_____. His cousin Weldon _____ for the _____from Wisconsin. Mike got_____ in _____ .

Weldon_____on Saturday. The two cousins_____their_____ .

The sheriff's deputy_____ their names. He_____the boys to _____ at the _____ location. It was_____that small_____caves _____be found in the hills_____New Braunfels. "You shouldn't be there _____very _____ ," the_____said. "Go _____ slowly, and be _____, boys."

Below a_____ limestone _____ , the two _____ saw a _____. A_____ was suddenly_____ by Mike. The boys _____ a draft of_____ air coming _____ the rock and_____. As they_____ , they were_____ by small rocks.

Further_____ revealed a _____ downward passage which _____into a _____.

Suddenly, Weldon _____ his _____ . The _____ fell _____. Weldon did not_____ very _____. It was _____without the _____ , but Weldon _____ his way_____ .

Mike_____half an hour_____accompanied by two_____deputies. The officers_____ already_____ the hills for them. One of the deputies was _____ on a _____ladder. "It was an _____," Mike said.

Everything_____ fine. A rope was _____ round Weldon's_____ . Mike _____ to help. Soon,_____ emerged on the_____ . The deputy _____the _____ carefully. Everyone was _____.

V. *Grammar and Syntax* *(Points of Interest)*

A. The Passive Voice

Until now we have used the ACTIVE voice. The *doer* of the action was the *subject* in the ACTIVE VOICE. The one who was acted upon, the RECEIVER, was the *object*. In the PASSIVE VOICE, the original RECEIVER becomes the *subject,* and the original *doer* of the action becomes the object of the preposition *by.*

Active Voice: Mike (*doer* of the action) discovered a cave (*receiver* of the action).

Passive Voice: A cave (*receiver* of the action) was discovered by Mike (*doer* of the action).

Active Voice: Small falling rocks (*doers* of the action) hit the climbing explorers (*receivers* of the action).

Passive Voice: The explorers (*receivers* of the action) were hit by small falling rocks (*doers* of the action).

— — — — — — — — — — — — — — — — — — — —

B.   The Imperative Mood

The IMPERATIVE MOOD can be expressed by a *simple verb* form. It expresses *commands, requests,* or *instructions.*

1. Singular and plural, second person (the subject *you* is understood):
   Take a train.
   Don't take a train.   (negative)
   Bring a sleeping bag.
   Don't bring a sleeping bag.   (negative)

2. First and second person together:
   Let's get down lower.
   Let's not get down lower.   (negative)

   Let's see what's down there.
   Let's not see what's down there.   (negative)

3. An adverb of frequency may precede the imperative verb:
   Always descend carefully.
   Don't *ever* leave your lamp behind.

4. In direct address, a noun may precede the imperative verb, or it may follow it:

Mike, hand me the rope.
Hand me the rope, *Mike.*

5. The pronoun *you* is often used, as in the following imperative sentences:
    a. To get down, *you* must use the rope.
    Don't *you* forget it.

    b. *You* must be careful.
    You shouldn't be there alone.
    You will see the light at the other end.

6. To ask earnestly, entreat, you use the verb *do:*
    Do be careful down there.
    Do take precautions.

7. Words of politeness sometimes precede or follow the imperative verb in a request.
    Please, hand me the lamp.

    $\begin{matrix} Will \\ Would \end{matrix}$ *you (please)* remember the light?

    Go down slowly, *please.*

    Remember to come next summer, *please.*

    Stop the noise, $\begin{matrix} will \\ would \end{matrix}$ *you (please)?*

8. Some commands appear as printed signs or slogans:
    NO SMOKING   KEEP OFF THE GRASS
    DO NOT ENTER   KEEP OUT
    RIGHT TURN ONLY   NO PARKING

VI. *Word Recognition*

A. Circle the word (phrase) in Column II most *like* the word in Column I, and circle the word (phrase) in Column III most *unlike* the word in Column I. This oral identification of words ought to be timed.

COLUMN I		COLUMN II		COLUMN III
1. **accompany**	a.	escort	a.	lack
	b.	help	b.	hinder
	c.	carry	c.	leave
2. **assume**	a.	possess	a.	know
	b.	suppose	b.	hinder
	c.	carry	c.	sell
3. **broad**	a.	warm	a.	far
	b.	wide	b.	narrow
	c.	hot	c.	unsafe
4. **careless**	a.	sudden	a.	careful
	b.	abrupt	b.	usual
	c.	reckless	c.	married
5. **crawl**	a.	carry	a.	run
	b.	creep	b.	work
	c.	relax	c.	hinder
6. **dark**	a.	indicative	a.	plain
	b.	obscure	b.	light
	c.	undecided	c.	narrow
7. **deep**	a.	big	a.	creeping
	b.	buried	b.	excavated
	c.	vague	c.	shallow
8. **dig**	a.	argue	a.	bury
	b.	expose	b.	ignore
	c.	excavate	c.	assume
9. **discover**	a.	find	a.	assume
	b.	locate	b.	suppose
	c.	place	c.	search
10. **explore**	a.	investigate	a.	behave
	b.	sell	b.	ignore
	c.	cross	c.	work
11. **hasten**	a.	overturn	a.	slow down

		b.	quicken	b.	control
		c.	tip over	c.	regulate
12.	**immediately**	a.	so on	a.	after a while
		b.	at once	b.	specifically
		c.	haltingly	c.	lacking
13.	**indicated**	a.	halted	a.	concealed
		b.	dragged	b.	sold
		c.	specified	c.	unspecified
14.	**look forward to**	a.	go down	a.	hinder
		b.	anticipate	b.	purchase
		c.	stop	c.	dread
15.	**multiply**	a.	suppose	a.	decrease
		b.	argue	b.	discover
		c.	increase	c.	expose
16.	**narrow**	a.	small	a.	wide
		b.	tight	b.	straight
		c.	large	c.	vast
17.	**precaution**	a.	care	a.	disorder
		b.	profession	b.	worry
		c.	task	c.	carelessness
18.	**preparation**	a.	precaution	a.	disorder
		b.	arrangement	b.	disclosure
		c.	care	c.	carelessness
19.	**pull**	a.	tow	a.	work
		b.	run	b.	cross
		c.	bring	c.	push
20.	**release**	a.	answer	a.	confine
		b.	free	b.	damage
		c.	examine	c.	assure
21.	**reveal**	a.	disclose	a.	break
		b.	discover	b.	hide
		c.	support	c.	joke
22.	**search**	a.	release	a.	halt

	b. find	b.	close
	c. continue	c.	discover

23. **spread**
   - a. rescue
   - b. separate
   - c. endanger
   - a. converge
   - b. save
   - c. lower

24. **trouble**
   - a. difficulty
   - b. recklessness
   - c. chore
   - a. pleasure
   - b. order
   - c. precaution

25. **twisting**
   - a. broad
   - b. curving
   - c. wide
   - a. straight
   - b. narrow
   - c. deep

26. **warn**
   - a. yell
   - b. shout
   - c. caution
   - a. encourage
   - b. practice
   - c. listen

B. In the space on the left write the word(s) that would best fit the expression in **bold print**. Make other necessary changes. Read aloud.

_____ 1. The children **anticipated** the annual trip.

_____ 2. Mike got interested in **cave exploring.**

_____ 3. Weldon is an experienced **spelunker.**

_____ 4. They began their preparations **at once.**

_____ 5. Stay at the indicated **place.**

_____ 6. It was **assumed** there were caves.

_____ 7. The deputy had a **wide** grin.

_____ 8. There was a large **bedrock** bridge.

_____ 9. The boys **excavated** further.

_____10. They felt a cool **current** of air.

_____11. It came through the **rubble.**

_____12. There was a **curving** passage.

_____13. The explorers **crept** through the passage.

_____14. Mike handed Weldon the **cord.**

_____ 15. The noise **reproduced** itself with an echo.

_____ 16. The flashlight **ended its fall** below.

_____ 17. Weldon's voice came **plainly** from below.

_____ 18. His foot was **wedged** between two rocks.

_____ 19. He thought his ankle was **broken.**

_____ 20. Don't **josh**, Mike, go get help!

_____ 21. Mike returned **escorted** by two deputies.

_____ 22. The deputy was **lowered** on a rope ladder.

_____ 23. A rope was **secured** round his waist.

_____ 24. They **towed** him upward.

_____ 25. The deputy **freed** his foot.

_____ 26. Everybody **came out** on the surface.

VII. *Concept Recognition*

Fill in the most appropriate word (phrase) to express the CONCEPT of the sentence according to the narrative. Read the complete sentence aloud.

A. The Campbell children looked forward to _____ .

1. the annual trip 2. the planning
3. thinking 4. the summer

B. When they get careless, even adults _____ .

1. investigate 2. explore
3. get in trouble 4. ignore

C. Mike assured his parents that he would _____ .

1. anticipate the trip 2. be careful
3. find a cave 4. be careless

D. When Weldon arrived, the two cousins began their _____ .

1. preparations 2. trip
3. exploration 4. pleasure

E.   They took sleeping bags because_____ .

    1. Mrs. Campbell cautioned   2. it gets cold in the hills
    3. they took a lamp   4. they were experienced

F.   If they haven't shown up in three days, the deputies would_____ .

    1. come up to get them   2. take precautions
    3. be surprised   4. plan a trip

G.   When they felt a current of cool air coming through the rock, they found

_____ .

    1. a bear   2. a passage
    3. a bridge   4. a way back

H.   Weldon demanded a rope because he wanted _____ .

    1. to get down   2. to climb
    3. to get ready   4. to explore

I.   The flashlight fell when Weldon _____ .

    1. tied the rope   2. lost his footing.
    3. looked up   4. talked

J.   Weldon was unable to move because _____.

    1. he fell very far   2. he yelled loud
    3. his foot was wedged   4. his ankle was fractured
       between rocks.

K.   A rope was tied round Weldon's waist to _____ .

    1. pull him up   2. secure his descent
    3. keep him in place   4. help him explore

L.   The deputy spread the rocks to _____.

    1. explore them   2. release Weldon's foot
    3. examine them   4. lower Mike

VIII.   *Telling the Meaning*

A.   Place a check mark (✓) in front of the word in COLUMN II that best fits the MEANING of the word in COLUMN I. Read aloud a complete sentence using this word.

COLUMN I   COLUMN II

1. **accident**   _____ a. search
                           _____ b. mishap
                           _____ c. plan

2. **anticipate**   _____ a. look forward to
                           _____ b. dread
                           _____ c. explore

3. **arrangement**   _____ a. preparation
                           _____ b. chance
                           _____ c. unpreparedness

4. **buried**   _____ a. deep
                           _____ b. modest
                           _____ c. shallow

5. **care**   _____ a. design
                           _____ b. carelessness
                           _____ c. precaution

6. **caution**   _____ a. encourage
                           _____ b. warn
                           _____ c. explore

7. **creep**   _____ a. crawl
                           _____ b. run
                           _____ c. gain

8. **curving**   _____ a. uneven terrain
                           _____ b. straight
                           _____ c. twisting

9. **difficulty**   _____ a. order
                           _____ b. pleasure
                           _____ c. trouble

10. **disclose**   _____ a. hide
                            _____ b. discover
                            _____ c. reveal

11. **escort**   _____ a.   be alone
                                     _____ b.   accompany
                                     _____ c.   relax

12. **excavate**   _____ a.   dig
                                     _____ b.   bury
                                     _____ c.   compensate

13. **fracture**   _____ a.   shout
                                     _____ b.   mend
                                     _____ c.   break

14. **halt**   _____ a.   close
                                     _____ b.   continue
                                     _____ c.   end

15. **investigate**   _____ a.   ignore
                                     _____ b.   warn
                                     _____ c.   explore

16. **look for**   _____ a.   carry
                                     _____ b.   search
                                     _____ c.   discover

17. **obscure**   _____ a.   dark
                                     _____ b.   light
                                     _____ c.   moist

18. **reckless**   _____ a.   careful
                                     _____ b.   careless
                                     _____ c.   unafraid

19. **rescue**   _____ a.   let down
                                     _____ b.   endanger
                                     _____ c.   save

20. **show**   _____ a.   indicate
                                     _____ b.   conceal
                                     _____ c.   behave

21. **suppose**   _____ a.   argue
                                     _____ b.   assume
                                     _____ c.   know

22. **tight**
      _____ a.   distant
      _____ b.   narrow
      _____ c.   wide

23. **wedge**
      _____ a.   release
      _____ b.   constrict
      _____ c.   comfort

24. **wide**
      _____ a.   simple
      _____ b.   broad
      _____ c.   narrow

B. Return to Exercise A. Place two check marks (//) in front of the word in COLUMN II that is the ANTONYM of the word in COLUMN I. Read aloud a complete sentence using this word.

C. Select one of the three (3) words (phrases) that best fulfills the MEANING of the sentence according to the narrative. Insert the word in the blank space. Read the completed sentence aloud.

1. The Campbells were thinking about vacation because_____.
   a. summer came   b. they liked   c. they planned
                              exploring

2. Mike didn't look forward to a family trip because he_____.
   a. was unhappy   b. didn't like   c. planned a vacation
                           summer   of his own

3. Mrs. Campbell cautioned Mike because she_____.
   a. was happy   b. cared   c. took precautions

4. Mike got interested in spelunking when_____.
   a. he heard about the   b. he heard that   c. he heard about
       hills   Weldon was   caves
                       exploring caves

5. Mike was sure they would take precautions because_____.
   a. Weldon was coming   b. the deputy was   c. Weldon was an
                         there   experienced
                                spelunker

6. The deputies would come up to get the boys_____ .
   a. after three days   b. when they asked c. when they
                              for help   discovered the
                                                    cave

7. A cave was discovered by Mike when_____ .
   a. they fell inside   b. the boys felt a   c. the rocks hit them
                              draft of cool air

8. Weldon demanded the rope. He wanted to_____ .
   a. descend   b. climb   c. crawl

9. There was a loud noise when the lamp_____ .
   a. came to a halt   b. hit the walls   c. stopped falling

10. Weldon was unable to ascend because_____ .
    a. he had no lamp   b. he was unhappy   c. his foot was wedged
                                                  in between two rocks

11. Mike was lucky because the officers were_____ .
    a. in New Braunfels   b. already searching c. came to the cave
                              the hills

12. To get Weldon out, they had to_____ .
    a. tie a rope round his b. search the hills c. lower the ladder for
       waist   him

13. To get Weldon's foot free, the deputy_____ .
    a. spread the rope   b. spread the rocks c. pulled him up

14. Everybody emerged happy because_____ .
    a. Weldon's ankle was b. they saw the   c. Mike was a spelunker
       only sprained   grizzly

IX.   *Comprehension   [Exercises]*

A.   Place a check mark (✓) in front of the correct response to each of the statements according to the narrative.

   1. The Campbells looked forward to

      _____a. the annual family trip.

_____ b. spelunking.
_____ c. Weldon's visit.

2. Mike was planning

_____ a. a trip with the family.
_____ b. a vacation of his own.
_____ c. a trip to Wisconsin.

3. Mrs. Campbell warned Mike about

_____ a. going on vacation.
_____ b. exploring caves.
_____ c. his cousin Weldon.

4. Mike acted hurt because

_____ a. Mrs. Campbell cared.
_____ b. Mrs. Campbell warned him.
_____ c. Weldon didn't arrive.

5. When did Weldon arrive?

_____ a. on Sunday.
_____ b. on Saturday.
_____ c. on Monday.

6. Why did Weldon bring a sleeping bag?

_____ a. because it gets cold in the hills
_____ b. because the cave is deep.
_____ c. because he wanted to sleep.

7. The deputies would come up to get the boys

_____ a. if they called the sheriff.
_____ b. if they got lost.
_____ c. if they didn't show up in three days.

8. What was discovered by Mike?

_____ a. a cave.
_____ b. a draft.
_____ c. a rock.

9. What hit the boys as they descended?

_____ a. the draft.

_____ b. the small falling rocks.

_____ c. the lamp.

10. To get down lower, Weldon needed

     _____ a. a lamp and a rope.

     _____ b. a ladder.

     _____ c. a sleeping bag.

11. Weldon could not come up because

     _____ a. he found a cave.

     _____ b. his foot was wedged in between rocks.

     _____ c. he had no ladder.

12. What did Weldon find in the cave?

     _____ a. a man.

     _____ b. a lamp.

     _____ c. a skeleton.

13. Why was Weldon glad?

     _____ a. he heard a grizzly.

     _____ b. he heard voices.

     _____ c. he saw the deputies.

14. To get Weldon up, they

     _____ a. tied a rope round his waist.

     _____ b. gave him a rope.

     _____ c. gave him a lamp.

15. To release Weldon's foot, the deputy

     _____ a. pulled.

     _____ b. spread the rocks.

     _____ c. pushed.

16. What did the deputy say?

     _____ a. Weldon's foot was fractured.

     _____ b. Weldon's lamp was broken.

     _____ c. Weldon's ankle was sprained.

B. Below there are three (3) different thoughts expressed in each of the exercises. Assign the proper sequence (order of THOUGHT, according to the narrative, by numbering 1 to 3. Read aloud.

1. a. the Campbells were thinking   _____
    b. when summer came   _____
    c. about vacation   _____

2. a. the annual family trip   _____
    b. looked forward to   _____
    c. the children   _____

3. a. get into trouble   _____
    b. even adults   _____
    c. when they get careless   _____

4. a. as planned   _____
    b. on Saturday   _____
    c. Weldon arrived   _____

5. a. took down their names   _____
    b. the sheriff's deputy   _____
    c. in New Braunfels   _____

6. a. to stay   _____
    b. at the indicated location   _____
    c. he also asked the boys   _____

7. a. it was assumed that small   _____
    b. be found in the hills   _____
    c. undiscovered caves could   _____

8. a. the two explorers saw a hole   _____
    b. below a large   _____
    c. limestone bridge   _____

9. a. by small falling rocks   _____
    b. they were hit   _____
    c. as they descended,   _____

10. a. further digging revealed   _____
    b. which opened into a cave   _____
    c. a twisting, downward passage   _____

11. a. use the rope   _____

   b. you must   _____
   c. to get down   _____

12. a. throughout with an echo   _____
    b. as it hit against the walls,   _____
    c. the noise multiplied   _____

13. a. somewhere deep below   _____
    b. hit bottom   _____
    c. finally, the lamp   _____

14. a. as Mike listened anxiously   _____
    b. his voice came   _____
    c. clearly from below   _____

15. a. the lamp, but Weldon   _____
    b. felt his way around him   _____
    c. it was dark without   _____

16. a. accompanied by sheriff's deputies   _____
    b. half an hour later   _____
    c. Mike returned   _____

17. a. he was lucky the officers   _____
    b. for them as they'd promised   _____
    c. were already searching the hills   _____

18. a. Weldon was glad   _____
    b. voices above   _____
    c. to hear   _____

19. a. with Mike's help, pulled   _____
    b. Weldon carefully upward   _____
    c. the deputy above,   _____

20. a. releasing Weldon's ankle   _____
    b. the rocks with a crowbar,   _____
    c. below, the deputy spread   _____

21. a. examined   _____
    b. the deputy   _____
    c. the injury carefully   _____

C. There are some statements listed below about the narrative. Write **T** for **True** in front of each statement that you think is true. Write **F** for **False** if the statement is not true. Read aloud.

_____ 1. The children looked forward to the family trip.

_____ 2. Mike looked forward to the family trip.

_____ 3. Weldon was a spelunker.

_____ 4. Mrs. Campbell warned Mike.

_____ 5. Mike didn't act hurt.

_____ 6. Weldon arrived on Monday.

_____ 7. It gets cold in the hills.

_____ 8. To explore caves you must have a lamp.

_____ 9. The deputy wrote down their names.

_____ 10. There were caves in the hills.

_____ 11. There was a hole below a limestone bridge.

_____ 12. A cave was discovered by Weldon.

_____ 13. A draft of cool air came through the rocks.

_____ 14. The boys were hit by small rocks.

_____ 15. Weldon was excited.

_____ 16. A passage opened into a cave.

_____ 17. Suddenly Mike lost his footing.

_____ 18. The lamp fell downward.

_____ 19. The falling lamp made a noise.

_____ 20. Weldon fell very far.

_____ 21. In the cave he found a skeleton.

_____ 22. The skeleton was that of a man.

_____ 23. An accident can happen to anybody.

_____ 24. Everyone was happy.

_____ 25. The deputy pulled Weldon upward.

_____ 26. Weldon's ankle was fractured.

X.   *Composition and Discussion*

A.   In Column I are beginnings of sentences. In Column II are the completions
to sentences of Column I. Select the completion best fitting each sentence
in Column I according to the narrative. Read the completed sentences
orally. Compose new sentences orally and discuss the narrative.

COLUMN I   COLUMN II

1. The children looked forward . . . .   a. his parents.
2. His cousin Weldon . . . .   b. as planned.
3. Even adults get into trouble . . . . .   c. crawled through a labyrinth.
4. Mike assured . . . .   d. without the lamp.
5. Weldon arrived on Saturday . . . . .   e. somewhere deep below.
6. Below a large bridge . . . .   f. very far.
7. A cave was suddenly . . . .   g. already searching the hills.
8. The two explorers . . . .   h. was lowered on a rope ladder.
9. The lamp hit bottom . . . .   i. when they get careless.
10. Weldon did not fall . . . .   j. the two explorers saw a hole.
11. It was dark . . . .   k. half an hour later.
12. Mike returned . . . .   l. discovered by Mike.
13. The officers were . . . .   m. emerged on the surface.
14. One of the deputies . . . .   n. to the annual family trip.
15. Soon, everybody . . . .   o. was coming from Wisconsin.

B.   1. Describe a cave.
2. What do you need for exploring caves?
3. Tell us about Mike's and Weldon's trip.
4. Tell us about the rescue.

C.   Read this poem aloud. Answer orally the questions listed following the
poem.

They say. . .

He speaks, and it is done.
He makes things grow up high
into the sky, and down
deep into the ground. . .

He says, "Let there be light!"
And it is light. And darkness
follows, for both
are part of life. . .

Yet too much rain
will ravage[1] in a flood, while   [1] destroy
the burning sun can
parch[2] this fertile earth. . .   [2] dry

They say that man is blinded
by excessive[3] light, and only   [3] too much
the shade brings him
the longed for[4] rest. . .   [4] needed

1. Identify the *imperative* in this poem.
2. Identify the *passive* in this poem.
3. Discuss the meaning of the second stanza.
4. What is the meaning of the words "light" and "darkness"?
5. What does the poem tell you? Discuss it in class.

D. Describe what you see in the picture below.

* * * * * *

Chapter Eight

Saving Face

Words to remember:

Past Perfect Continuous

had + been + Verb + ing

Sequence of Tenses
if — would
the following — the third, etc.

the in a *time*
or *space* sequence

I. *Narrative*

A.   His family was happy when Professor Stuart signed with the community college. The professor had been looking for a job since January. He was glad when he was offered the position of Chairman of the English Department.

B.   Now, the Stuarts went out to shop for a house. There was Professor John Stuart, his wife Lilian, and their two sons, Shawn and Kip. Mrs. Stuart was of Chinese descent. John Stuart married Lilian while they were students at

M.Y.U. It was the second year of college for him. John had been learning Chinese as a minor subject. Lilian was a student from Taiwan. Knowing Lilian improved John's knowledge of that difficult language. Some thought he had been speaking Chinese all his life because it was as good as Lilian's. But John knew he didn't speak as well as his wife. He was always trying hard to improve his knowledge of the language.

C.   Not far down the street from the Campbells a house was being sold. It was larger than the Stuarts needed. It was a big house and more expensive than they were able to afford. But John and Lilian liked the neighborhood. Besides, the professor had been meeting Mr. Campbell at social gatherings. They established a friendship immediately because Mr. Campbell had also studied at M.Y.U.

D.   The Stuarts moved into their new home on a Sunday. Moving is always a great chore. Some of the neighbors joined the Campbells in helping the Stuarts with their moving. They had been working hard when the Stuarts' next-door neighbor was overheard saying: "Why don't these foreigners stay out of our neighborhood?" No one answered. The Campbells were worried about the Stuarts who had been unaccustomed to prejudice. The neighbor said that the Stuarts might not live in the neighborhood for very long.

E.   The second month had gone by. Lilian Stuart received her U.S. citizenship on the twentieth of May. She had been living in the United States for five years by then. That's the required time for residence in the United States before an alien can become a citizen. The swearing-in ceremony was impressive. Mrs. Campbell cried, and Mr. Campbell was proud to have sponsored Lilian.

F.   The Stuarts planned a big neighborhood party to celebrate Lilian's citizenship. Her birthday fell on the twenty-fifth of May. They had been waiting for a proper occasion to celebrate. The only problem was Mrs. Fox, the unfriendly neighbor.

G.   Lilian learned that the Foxes were going to be away on the twenty-seventh of May. "That's the night I'll give the party," she told John. Her husband didn't always understand Lilian's ways, but he loved her, and he trusted her judgment.

H.   The neighbors had been celebrating Lilian's new citizenship throughout the night. The party was a great success. Everyone was happy to welcome the new American. No one missed the Foxes. Only John saw a mysterious twinkle in Lilian's eyes.

I.   On the following day Mrs. Fox dropped in at the Stuarts' home. "I must apologize for missing your party, Lilian," she called Mrs. Stuart by her first name. "I am happy you have come to tell me this, Gertrude," Lilian responded. "But. . .I don't understand . . ." Gertrude stammered. "Well, it's like this," Lilian went on. "When I found out you were going to be away, I decided to give a party. I planned this to give you a chance not to come. But I had hoped you'd come to apologize, as you did. If you hadn't done this, I'd have given you another chance, and another one after that, until you would understand. I'm glad you came; if not my party would have been in vain."

J.   Mrs. Fox suddenly understood. So this is what they call "saving face"? "How wonderful of you, Lilian, to give me this chance!" she exclaimed. "To do a thing like this you must really care for people! I would come, if you gave me another chance." Gertrude blushed, embarrassed. She embraced the new American heartily. They were going to be friends now. "On second thought," Lilian said with a broad smile, "I wouldn't have missed this for anything."

* * *

II.   *Words in Context   [Pictographs]*

Below are some of the words used in the narrative. Where possible, each word has a **[synonym]** , or it is defined as used in the story. Where possible, an (*antonym*) is also given. Make up sentences about the pictographs choosing the words you need. Read aloud.

Example: **[improve]** = The Stuarts bettered their position.

A, B, C, and D.

sign **[contract]** ; position **[post]** ; shop for **[select]** (*sell*); descent **[origin]** ; minor **[secondary]** (*major*); improve **[better]** (*worsen*); sell **[trade for money]** (*buy*); afford **[have the money for]** ; establish **[secure]** (*break up*)

E, F, G and H.

required **[necessary]** (*unnecessary*); residence **[habitation]** ; alien **[immigrant]** (*citizen*); ceremony **[ritual]** ; impressive **[imposing]** (*unimpressive*); sponsor **[support]** ; celebrate **[observe festivities joyfully]** ; proper **[appropriate]** (*improper*); occasion **[opportunity]** ; problem **[difficulty]** (*solution*); trust **[have faith]** (*mistrust*)

I. and J.

following **[next]** (*previous*); drop in **[visit]** (*depart*); apologize **[express regret[** (*blame*); stammer **[stutter]** ; decide **[resolve]** (*hesitate*); save **[redeem]** (*lose*); embarrass **[perplex]** (*relieve*); embrace **[hug]** (*recoil*); heartily **[sincerely[** (*insincerely*)

Drawing of paragraphs A, B, C, & D

III. Structures [Phrases]

Below are some PHRASES taken from the narrative. Make complete sentences and read them aloud.

A.	with	—	the	—	Community College
B.	looking	—	for	—	a job
C.	position	—	of	—	chairman
D.	out	—	to	—	shop
E.	for	—	a	—	house
F.	of	—	Chinese	—	descent
G.	students	—	at	—	M.Y.U.
H.	the	—	second	—	year
I.	a	—	minor	—	subject
J.	that	—	difficult	—	language

Drawing of paragraphs E, F, G, and H

K.	all	—	his	—	life
L.	to	—	improve	—	his knowledge
M.	down	—	the	—	street
N.	it	—	was	—	larger
O.	a	—	big	—	house
P.	more	—	expensive		
Q.	able	—	to	—	afford
R.	at	—	social	—	gatherings
S.	also	—	studied	—	at M.Y.U.
T.	their	—	new	—	home
U.	a	—	great	—	chore
V.	next	—	door	—	neighbor
W.	unaccustomed	—	to	—	prejudice
X.	the	—	twentieth	—	of May
Y.	time	—	for	—	residence
Z.	the	—	unfriendly	—	neighbor

Drawing of paragraphs I & J

IV. Sentences

A. Read the following sentences aloud. Repeat, substituting where possible, the synonym of the word in *italics.*

Example: His family liked the new *position.*
His family was happy when he had gotten the new *post.*

1. Professor Stuart *signed* with the Community College.
2. The professor had been *shopping* for a job.
3. He was offered a *position.*
4. The Stuarts went to *select* a house.
5. John had been *improving* his knowledge of Chinese.
6. John was *trying* to improve his knowledge.
7. A house was being *sold.*
8. It was larger than the one they *required.*
9. They could *afford* the neighborhood.

10. They *established* a friendship.
11. The Stuarts moved into their new *residence.*
12. Moving is always a great *chore.*
13. The Stuarts had been unaccustomed to *prejudice.*
14. They *planned* a neighborhood party.
15. They had been waiting to *celebrate* her citizenship.
16. The only *problem* was Mrs. Fox.
17. He *trusted* her judgment.
18. Everyone *dropped* in to celebrate.
19. John saw a *mysterious* twinkle in her eyes.
20. Mrs. Fox *appeared* at the Stuarts' home.
21. Mrs. Fox suddenly *understood.*

B.   Fill in the blanks with words from the narrative. Each space may be filled by a word or phrase. Do not refer back to the narrative. Where possible, use variations of the missing words. Read aloud.

The_____ was _____ . Professor Stuart_____ with the Community College. The professor had _____ for a_____ . He was _____ a _____.

The Stuarts went out to _____ for a _____ . John Stuart _____ Lilian at M.Y.U. It was the _____ year of _____ for_____ . John had been _____ Chinese. Lilian was a _____ from Taiwan. John was _____ to _____ his knowledge.

A _____ was being _____ . It was _____than what they_____ . It was a _____ house. They_____the _____ . They _____ a _____.

The Stuarts_____ into their_____ home. Moving is _____ a great _____ . The Stuarts had been _____ to _____.

The_____ month had gone by. Lilian _____ her U.S. _____ . She had been_____in the United States for five_____by _____. That's the _____ time for _____ in the United States before an _____ can _____ a citizen.

They_____ a _____ party. They had been _____ to _____. The only _____was Mrs. Fox, the _____neighbor.

The Foxes were going to be _____. "I'll give a_____ that_____." Her _____ didn't _____ understand her. But he_____ her, and he _____ her _____.

The_____ had been _____ Lilian's new _____ throughout the night. The _____ was a great _____ . Everyone was _____ to _____ the new_____.

Mrs. Fox_____ at the Stuarts'_____ . "I'm_____ you came; if not my _____ would have been in _____," Lilian said.

Mrs. Fox_____ understood. She _____the new American. They were going to be_____ now. "I wouldn't have _____ this for _____," Lilian said.

V.   *Grammar and Syntax   (Points of Interest)*

A.   The **Past Perfect Continuous** tells about an *action* or a *condition* that takes place *up to a certain time* in the past. We use the forms: *had + been + verb + ing*

> The professor *had been looking* for a job.
> John *had been learning* Chinese.
> Some thought he *had been speaking* Chinese all his life.
> The professor *had been meeting* Mr. Campbell at social gatherings.
> They *had been waiting* for a proper occasion to celebrate.
> The neighbors *had been celebrating* Lilian's citizenship throughout the
> night.

— — — — — — — — — — — — — — — — — — —

B.   The **Sequence of Tenses** occurs most often in Noun Clauses.

If the MAIN VERB is in the PAST TENSE, it is often accompanied by a PAST VERB in the dependent clause.

A MAIN VERB in any other tense does not require a special verb form in the dependent clause.

MAIN VERB	in the PRESENT	in the PAST
Adverbial Clause	The Stuarts are *staying* here because they *are* my friends.	The man *stayed here* because he *was* ill.
Adjective Clause	The Campbells *are* worried about the Stuarts who *have been* unaccustomed to prejudice.	The Campbells *were worried* about the Stuarts who *had been* unaccustomed to prejudice.
Noun Clause	The neighbor *says* that the Stuarts *may* not *live* in this neighborhood for very long.	The neighbor *said* that the Stuarts *might* not *live* in this neighborhood for very long.

— — — — — — — — — — — — — — — — — — —

C.   More uses of *the.*

    1. *The* is frequently used with **ordinal numbers**:

        It was the second year of college for him.
        The second month had gone by.
        Lilian Stuart received her U.S. citizenship on *the twentieth of May.*
        Her birthday fell on *the twenty-fifth* of May.
        The Foxes were gong to be away on *the twenty-seventh* of May.

    2. *The* can also be used with **Adjectives** in a *time* or *space* sequence:

        On *the following* day Mrs. Fox appeared at the Stuarts' home.

        —

D. *Would* is used in **conditional** clauses.

        "*If* you hadn't done this, *I'd* have given you another chance."
        "I'm glad you came; *if* not, my party *would* have been in vain."
        "I *would* come if you gave me another chance."

VI.   *Word Recognition*

A.   Circle the word(s) in Column II most *like* the word in Column I, and circle
the word(s) in Column III most *unlike* the word in Column I. This oral
identification of words ought to be timed.

COLUMN I		COLUMN II		COLUMN III
1. **afford**	a.	have the money for	a.	need
	b.	practice	b.	misbehave
	c.	listen	c.	retain
2. **apologize**	a.	declare	a.	repress
	b.	express regret	b.	be wrong
	c.	testify	c.	blame
3. **decide**	a.	resolve	a.	precede
	b.	testify	b.	hesitate
	c.	affirm	c.	avoid

4. **embarrass**
    a. dominate
    b. perplex
    c. separate

    a. relieve
    b. advise
    c. counsel

5. **establish**
    a. control
    b. secure
    c. detain

    a. let go
    b. tip over
    c. break up

6. **following**
    a. beyond
    b. next
    c. farther

    a. previous
    b. near
    c. orderly

7. **heartily**
    a. sincerely
    b. sympathetic
    c. kind

    a. court
    b. unkind
    c. insincere

8. **impressive**
    a. wealthy
    b. imposing
    c. protected

    a. unimpressive
    b. unsafe
    c. usual

9. **improve**
    a. rest
    b. better
    c. listen

    a. hinder
    b. worsen
    c. lack

10. **minor**
    a. secondary
    b. happy
    c. grumpy

    a. at rest
    b. major
    c. active

11. **problem**
    a. opportunity
    b. chore
    c. difficulty

    a. solution
    b. task
    c. trust

12. **proper**
    a. modest
    b. appropriate
    c. simple

    a. improper
    b. protected
    c. distant

13. **save**
    a. assure
    b. succeed
    c. redeem

    a. lose
    b. ignore
    c. dominate

14. **sell**
    a. sink
    b. work
    c. trade for money

    a. buy
    b. stop
    c. rest

15. **shop**	a.	cross	a.	work
	b.	behave	b.	take
	c.	select	c.	sell
16. **trust**	a.	possess	a.	hinder
	b.	have faith	b.	mistrust
	c.	help	c.	lack

B.   In the space on the left write the word(s) that best fit the expression in **bold print**. Make other necessary changes. Read aloud.

_____ 1. The professor was offered a **position**.

_____ 2. The Stuarts went out to **select** a house.

_____ 3. Lilian was of Chinese **origin**.

_____ 4. John's **secondary subject** was Chinese.

_____ 5. They **secured** a friendship.

_____ 6. Five years of **habitation** are **necessary**.

_____ 7. An **alien** becomes a citizen.

_____ 8. The **formality** of swearing-in was **impressive**.

_____ 9. Mr. Campbell **supported** Lilian's citizenship.

_____ 10. The neighbors **observed** Lilian's citizenship.

_____ 11. It was the **proper opportunity**.

_____ 12. John **had faith** in Lilian's judgment.

_____ 13. On the next day, Mrs. Fox **dropped in**.

_____ 14. She came to **excuse** herself.

_____ 15. Mrs. Fox **stuttered**.

_____ 16. Lilian **decided** to have a party.

_____ 17. Mrs. Fox **hugged** Lilian **heartily**.

VII.   *Concept Recognition*

Fill in the word (phrase) most fitting to express the concept of the sentence according to the narrative. Read the complete sentence aloud.

A. The Stuart family was happy when the professor _____ .

1. got a position
2. met the Campbells
3. learned Chinese
4. looked for a job

B. John Stuart knew his knowledge of Chinese was _____ .

1. as good as Lilian's
2. not as good as Lilian's
3. better than Lilian's
4. as good as it could be

C. He worked hard to _____ .

1. improve his friendship
2. be a good chairman
3. improve his knowledge of the language
4. learn more about Lilian

D. They bought a bigger house than they needed because _____ .

1. the Foxes lived there.
2. they liked the neighborhood
3. they met at social gatherings
4. Lilian liked to give parties

E. Some neighbors helped the Stuarts with their moving because _____ .

1. they liked the Campbells
2. they were next-door neighbors.
3. moving is a great chore
4. they studied at M.Y.U.

F. With her remark, Mrs. Fox showed _____ .

1. her prejudice
2. her friendship
3. her worry
4. her happiness

G. The Campbells were worried because the Stuarts might be _____ .

1. hurt by the prejudice
2. afraid
3. accustomed to prejudice
4. prejudiced like Mrs. Fox

H. Lilian waited five years in residence to receive her citizenship because _____ .

1. she was in Taiwan
2. she studied at M.Y.U.
3. she liked the United States
4. it is the required time

I. Mrs. Campbell cried at the ceremony because it _____ .

1. took a long time
2. was required
3. was impressive
4. was the twentieth of May

J. The Stuarts planned a big party to _____ .

1. celebrate Lilian's citizenship   2. invite Mrs. Fox
3. invite unfriendly neighbors   4. have fun

K.   Lilian planned the party when _____ .

1. it was her birthday   2. the Foxes were away
3. John was at the college   4. Kip and Shawn were at school

L.   John didn't always understand Lilian, but he _____ .

1. listened to her   2. had faith in himself
3. had faith in her   4. had faith in his judgment

M.   Mrs. Fox appeared at the Stuarts' home to _____ .

1. come to the party   2. apologize for missing the party
3. be prejudiced   4. speak to John

N.   Lilian was happy because she knew that _____ .

1. her party was not in vain   2. Mrs. Fox was prejudiced
3. she gave a good party   4. John was happy

O.   Mrs. Fox called Lilian by her first name to show _____ .

1. prejudice   2. friendship
3. worry   4. happiness

P.   Lilian gave Mrs. Fox a chance to _____ .

1. worry   2. be happy
3. be away   4. save face

Q.   Mrs. Fox realized that Lilian _____ .

1. really cared for people   2. was from Taiwan
3. loved John   4. gave good parties

VIII.   *Telling the Meaning*

A.   Place a check mark (✓) in front of the word in COLUMN II that best fits the MEANING of the word in COLUMN I. Read aloud a complete sentence using this word.

COLUMN I		COLUMN II

1. **appropriate**
   - _____ a. grumpy
   - _____ b. proper
   - _____ c. improper

2. **better**
   - _____ a. improve
   - _____ b. worsen
   - _____ c. learn

3. **difficulty**
   - _____ a. problem
   - _____ b. task
   - _____ c. solution

4. **embrace**
   - _____ a. recoil
   - _____ b. hug
   - _____ c. possess

5. **express regret**
   - _____ a. blame
   - _____ b. apologize
   - _____ c. resolve

6. **have faith**
   - _____ a. hold on
   - _____ b. trust
   - _____ c. mistrust

7. **imposing**
   - _____ a. unimpressive
   - _____ b. impressive
   - _____ c. unafraid

8. **next**
   - _____ a. previous
   - _____ b. following
   - _____ c. modest

9. **offer**
   - _____ a. present
   - _____ b. say
   - _____ c. withhold

10. **perplex**
    - _____ a. relieve
    - _____ b. relax
    - _____ c. confuse

11. **redeem**
    - _____ a. save

_____ b.	lose
_____ c.	own

12. **resolve**

_____ a.	hesitate
_____ b.	rule
_____ c.	decide

13. **secondary**

_____ a.	major
_____ b.	great
_____ c.	minor

14. **secure**

_____ a.	break up
_____ b.	establish
_____ c.	move

15. **select**

_____ a.	sell
_____ b.	shop
_____ c.	bring

16. **sincerely**

_____ a.	heartily
_____ b.	distant
_____ c.	insincerely

17. **trade for money**

_____ a.	take
_____ b.	sell
_____ c.	buy

B. Return to Exercise A. Place two check marks (✓✓) in front of the word in COLUMN II that is the ANTONYM of the word in COLUMN I. Read aloud a complete sentence using this word.

C. Select one of the three (3) words (phrases) that best fulfills the MEANING of the sentence according to the narrative. Insert the words in the blank space. Read the completed sentence aloud.

1. Professor Stuart signed with the Community College to _____.
   a. move   b. take a post   c. find a home

2. The Stuart family was happy because_____.
   a. of the new job   b. they moved   c. they got a home

3. The professor was glad when _____.
   a. he was with the   b. he was at the   c. he was offered a
      family   college   position

4. Knowing Lilian _____ John's knowledge of Chinese.
   a. improved   b. prejudiced   c. excited

5. The Stuarts liked the neighborhood because _____.
   a. they liked the house   b. they bought the   c. the Campbells were
                                   house   friends

6. The neighbors helped with the moving to _____.
   a. have great fun   b. detain the   c. make moving easy
                                   Stuarts

7. Mrs. Fox made the remark to show her _____ for foreigners.
   a. liking   b. dislike   c. love

8. The Campbells worried because the Stuarts were not _____ to prejudice.
   a. neighbors   b. good   c. accustomed

9. An alien has to reside in the United States for five years to _____.
   a. become a citizen   b. buy a house   c. become prejudiced

10. Mrs. Campbell cried at the swearing-in ceremony because _____.
    a. she liked Lilian   b. she saw Mrs. Fox   c. she was unhappy

11. To celebrate Lilian's citizenship, the Stuarts planned _____.
    a. a big party   b. to go on a trip   c. to have a problem

12. Mrs. Fox was a problem because she _____.
    a. went on a trip.   b. was prejudiced   c. wouldn't come

13. Lilian planned the party during Mrs. Fox's absence to _____.
    a. have fun   b. celebrate with   c. give Mrs. Fox
                                 other neighbors   a chance

14. Lilian was glad Mrs. Fox came to apologize because _____.
    a. the party was a   b. she liked Mrs.   c. she didn't like
        success   Fox   parties

15. Mrs. Fox understood that to do a thing like this Lilian really _____.
    a. liked parties   b. liked people   c. didn't like people

16. To give someone a chance in this situation meant _____.
    a. to give a party   b. to like people   c. to save face

IX.   Comprehension   [Exercises]

A.   Place a check mark (✓) in front of the correct response to each of the statements according to the narrative. Read the complete sentences aloud.

1. The Stuarts were happy because

_____ a. the professor signed with the college.
_____ b. they were moving.
_____ c. they bought a house.

2. After John signed with the college

_____ a. they gave a party.
_____ b. they went to shop for a house.
_____ c. they took a trip.

3. John met Lilian

_____ a. when they were students at M.Y.U.
_____ b. when he was in Taiwan.
_____ c. when she visited in the United States.

4. The Stuarts went out to

_____ a. move.
_____ b. shop for a house.
_____ c. plan a party.

5. They moved not far from

_____ a. the Campbells.
_____ b. the college.
_____ c. the neighborhood.

6. The professor and Mr. Campbell studied

_____ a. on Taiwan.
_____ b. at M.Y.U.
_____ c. law.

7. The neighbors helped the Stuarts

_____ a. at the college.
_____ b. with the party.
_____ c. with their moving.

8. Lilian planned a party to

_____ a. welcome Mrs. Fox.
_____ b. celebrate her citizenship.
_____ c. celebrate John's job.

9. The only problem was

_____ a. the neighbors.
_____ b. John's family.
_____ c. Mrs. Fox.

10. Lilian planned the party when

_____ a. the Foxes were away.
_____ b. the neighbors would come.
_____ c. the Campbells would come.

11. When the Foxes returned, Mrs. Fox

_____ a. came to talk with John.
_____ b. came to the party.
_____ c. came to apologize to Lilian.

12. Lilian wanted to give Mrs. Fox a chance to

_____ a. come to the party.
_____ b. save face.
_____ c. be present.

B. Below there are three (3) different thoughts in each of the exercises. Assign the proper sequence (order) of THOUGHT, according to the narrative, by numbering 1 to 3. Read aloud.

1. a. with the community college   _____
   b. when Professor Stuart signed   _____
   c. his family was happy   _____

2. a. had been looking   _____
   b. for a job since January   _____
   c. the professor   _____

3. a. while they were   _____
   b. John Stuart married Lilian   _____
   c. students at M.Y.U.   _____

4. a. it was the second
   b. for him
   c. year of college

5. a. as a minor subject
   b. learning Chinese
   c. John had been

6. a. John's knowledge of
   b. knowing Lilian improved
   c. that difficult language

7. a. he didn't speak
   b. but John knew
   c. as well as his wife

8. a. to improve his knowledge
   b. he was always trying hard
   c. of the language

9. a. from the Campbells
   b. a house was being sold
   c. not far down the street

10. a. than the
    b. it was larger
    c. Stuarts needed

11. a. and more expensive than
    b. they were able to afford
    c. it was a big house

12. a. meeting Mr. Campbell
    b. besides, the professor had been
    c. at social gatherings

13. a. into their new home
    b. the Stuarts moved
    c. on a Sunday

14. a. joined the Campbells in helping
    b. the Stuarts with their moving
    c. some of the neighbors

15. a. stay out of   _____
     b. why don't these foreigners   _____
     c. our neighborhood   _____

16. a. the Campbells were worried   _____
     b. had been unaccustomed to prejudice   _____
     c. about the Stuarts who   _____

17. a. her U.S. citizenship   _____
     b. Lilian received   _____
     c. on the twentieth of May   _____

18. a. a big neighborhood party   _____
     b. to celebrate Lilian's citizenship   _____
     c. the Stuarts planned   _____

19. a. for a proper occasion   _____
     b. they had been waiting   _____
     c. to celebrate   _____

20. a. were going to be away   _____
     b. Lilian learned that the Foxes   _____
     c. on the twenty-seventh of May   _____

21. a. celebrating Lilian's new citizenship   _____
     b. the neighbors had been   _____
     c. throughout the night   _____

22. a. the new American   _____
     b. everyone was happy   _____
     c. to welcome   _____

23. a. on the following day   _____
     b. at the Stuarts' home   _____
     c. Mrs. Fox appeared   _____

24. a. you must really   _____
     b. to do a thing like this   _____
     c. care for people   _____

25. a. going to be   _____
     b. they were   _____
     c. friends now   _____

C. There are some statements listed below about the narrative. Write **T** for **True** in front of each statement that you think is true. Write **F** for **False** if the statement is not true. Read aloud.

_____ 1. Professor Stuart got a job, and his family was happy.

_____ 2. The professor had been looking for a job since February.

_____ 3. He was offered the position of a chairman.

_____ 4. The Stuarts had two sons.

_____ 5. Lilian was of Chinese descent.

_____ 6. They got married while they were students.

_____ 7. John learned Chinese as a major subject.

_____ 8. They bought a house not far from the Campbells.

_____ 9. The house was not very expensive.

_____ 10. The professor met Mr. Campbell at the University.

_____ 11. The Stuarts moved on Monday.

_____ 12. The neighbors helped them move.

_____ 13. Moving is easy.

_____ 14. The Campbells weren't worried about the Stuarts.

_____ 15. The Stuarts had been accustomed to prejudice.

_____ 16. Lilian received her citizenship in March.

_____ 17. Mr. Campbell sponsored Lilian.

_____ 18. The Stuarts planned a big party.

_____ 19. Mrs. Fox was no problem.

_____ 20. Lilian gave the party when the Foxes were home.

_____ 21. The party was a great success.

_____ 22. Everyone missed the Foxes.

_____ 23. Mrs. Fox came to apologize for missing the party.

_____ 24. Lilian was glad about Mrs. Fox's visit.

_____ 25. Mrs. Fox and Lilian were going to be friends.

_____ 26. Mrs. Fox embraced Lilian.

X. *Composition and Discussion*

A. In COLUMN I are the beginnings of sentences. In COLUMN II are the completions to sentences of COLUMN I. Select the completion best fitting each sentence in COLUMN I according to the narrative. Read the completed sentences orally. Compose new sentences orally and discuss the narrative.

COLUMN I	COLUMN II
1. The professor had been looking . .	a. for a proper occasion.
2. He was glad	b. about the Stuarts.
3. The Stuarts went out	c. while they were students.
4. John married Lilian	d. when he was offered a position.
5. Lilian was a student	e. for a job since January.
6. It was larger than	f. a great chore.
7. John and Lilian	g. you must really care for people.
8. Moving is always	h. what the Stuarts needed.
9. Why don't these foreigners	i. from Taiwan.
10. The Campbells were worried	j. to welcome the new American.
11. Lilian received her citizenship . . .	k. a great success.
12. The Stuarts planned	l. Mrs. Fox appeared at the Stuarts.
13. They had been waiting	m. to be friends now.
14. The party was	n. to shop for a house.
15. Everyone was happy	o. liked the neighborhood.
16. On the following day	p. stay out of our neighborhood?
17. To do a thing like this	q. on the twentieth of May.
18. They were going	r. a big party to celebrate.

B. 1. Tell us about the neighborhood you live in.
    2. On what occasion would you celebrate?
    3. Do you like Lilian Stuart? Why?
    4. Do you like Mrs. Fox? Why?
    5. Describe the change in Mrs. Fox.
    6. Why was Lilian's plan to "save face" successful?

C. Read the poem aloud. Answer orally the questions listed following the poem.

Words

If I could express a thought the first time

I would refuse to repeat in vain.
Were I able to cut down a tree at one stroke,[1]   [1] blow of an ax
I would strike but once. .

but

When running the risk[2] of being misunderstood,   [2] chance
or leaving things unaccomplished,[3]   [3] not done
I would spare[4] neither words nor deeds. .   [4] omit

1. Why is the poem titled "Words"?
2. Read orally the lines containing "would." Explain their meaning.
3. Find *the + ordinal* and read orally the entire line.
4. How does line 3 of the first stanza relate to line 3 of the second stanza?
5. How does the first stanza relate to the second stanza? Discuss it in class.
6. Does the poem clearly convey the idea expressed in its title? Tell how it does, or how it doesn't.

D.   Describe what you see in the picture below.

* * * * * *

Chapter Nine

The Americans

Words to remember:

Relative Clauses—*who, whom, which, whose, that,* etc.

Relative Pronoun as Subject—**as Object as Modifier of Noun**

I. Narrative

A. Many people who wished to seek a new life sailed across the seven seas to the shores of the United States of America. More recently, the fastest jets transport the immigrants who come from almost every country of the earth to the United States. Though they are of different nationalities, religions, and social classes, they are bound by some common goals. Many come in search of freedom to worship that they find here. Some look for food, others for fortune. For those who come, the United States of America is still the land of opportunity.

B. Some people look for fertile land which they can settle on. Others seek a home in big and small cities of this vast country. They are awed by the

201

great distances that span the land. A person could travel three thousand miles across this country and no one asks questions. There are no borders to cross, no passports to present. The newcomers are happy with the people whom they meet in their new homeland. But this happiness is not altogether without some setbacks.

C.   The same human elements which accompanied them to the New World became great obstacles. They brought with them biased opinions, old traditions, ancient customs, and quite a few well-established prejudices. People of similar national backgrounds settled close to each other. The German immigrants created their own neighborhoods, as did the Poles, the Italians, the Irish, and many other nationalities and ethnic groups. For the most part, they were tolerant of each other's religious beliefs. Though they met in their daily endeavors, most of them refused to allow their children to associate or intermarry.

D.   But as the population increases, people come to live closer together. They learn to tolerate differences, and accept changes. They respect people whose backgrounds are unlike their own. They find it necessary to settle their differences peacefully, under the law of the land. Not everyone was born under equal circumstances. But every individual has the right to the "pursuit of his own happiness." This is an inalienable right of every American.

E.   The Americans are a proud people. They are proud of their heritage. They remember the Revolution and the birth of the Republic. They know that to live in a democracy means to suffer many sacrifices. The Americans are used to changes. They know how to make the best of a situation, and they adjust readily to changes.

F.   Their president whose authority they respect will lead them. The Americans vote to elect their leadership in free elections. If their elected leaders prove untrustworthy, they will not stay in office. The people will not vote for them again.

G.   The American people are hard-working and tough. But underneath that toughness, they are charitable. They are always ready to help their fellow man, near and far. This is the reason why so many come to this land called the United States of America. They, too, want to be called "Americans."

* * *

II.   *Words in Context*   *[Pictographs]*

Below are the words used in the narrative. Where possible, each word has a [synonym], or it is defined as used in the story. Where possible, an (*antonym*) is also given. Make up sentences about the pictographs choosing the words you need. Read aloud.

Example: [**sail**] = The immigrants traveled by boat.

A. and B.

Drawing of paragraphs A & B

sail [**travel by boat**] ; shore [**coastline**] (*ocean*); recently [**lately**] (*long ago*); immigrant [**settler**] (*emigrant*); worship [**pray**] (*blaspheme*); fortune [**wealth**] (*poverty*); settle [**establish oneself**] (*move on*); fertile [**fruitful**] (*arid*); awe [**reverence**] (*irreverence*); span [**extend**] ; border [**boundary**] (*interior*); setback [**obstacle**] (*advancement*)

C. and D.

ethnic [**cultural**] ; tolerant [**understanding**] (*intolerant*); belief [**faith**] (*disbelief*); endeavor [**work**] (*idleness*); associate [**be friends**] (*disassociate*); marry [**wed**] (*divorce*); settle [**pacify**] (*unsettle*); difference [**dissimilarity**] (*similarity*); respect [**regard**] (*abuse*); pursuit [**striving**] (*avoiding*); inalienable [**indisuptable**] (*disuptable*)

Drawing of paragraphs C & D

E. F. and G.

> proud **[self-satisfied]** (*ashamed*); heritage **[tradition]**; sacrifice **[loss]**
> (*profit*); adjust **[adapt]** (*disturb*); untrustworthy **[unreliable]**
> (*trustworthy*); tough **[able to take adversity]** (*soft*); underneath **[beneath]**
> (*above*); charitable **[benevolent]** (*selfish*)

III. *Structures   [Phrases]*

Below are some PHRASES taken from the narrative. Make complete
sentences and read them aloud.

A.	across	—	the	—	seas
B.	to	—	the	—	shores
C.	from	—	every	—	country
D.	to	—	the	—	United States

Drawing of paragraphs E, F & G.

E.	by	—	some	—	common goals
F.	in	—	search	—	of freedom
G.	those	—	who	—	come
H.	in	—	big	—	cities
I.	the	—	great	—	distances
J.	across	—	this	—	country
K.	borders	—	to	—	cross
L.	happy	—	with	—	the people
M.	in	—	their	—	new homeland
N.	without	—	some	—	setbacks
O.	to	—	the	—	New World
P.	of	—	similar	—	background
Q.	close	—	to	—	each other
R.	in	—	their	—	endeavor
S.	to	—	their	—	children
T.	people	—	whose	—	background
U.	necessary	—	to	—	settle

V.	under	–	equal	–	circumstances
W.	pursuit	–	of	–	happiness
X.	of	–	their	–	heritage
Y.	best	–	of	–	a situation
Z.	tough	–	and	–	charitable

IV. Sentences

A. Read the following sentences aloud. Repeat, substituting where possible, the synonym of the word in *italics*, or a phrase that explains the meaning. Make other necessary changes.

Example: *Recently,* they travel by jet.
          Lately, the settlers come by jet.

1. People wished to *seek* a new life.
2. They *sailed* across the seas.
3. The *immigrants* come from almost every country.
4. They are of different *nationalities*.
5. Many come in search of *freedom*.
6. Others look for *fortune*.
7. The United States is the land of *opportunity*.
8. Some settle on *fertile* land.
9. They are *awed* by the great distances.
10. There are no *borders* to cross.
11. The *newcomers* are happy.
12. But there are some *setbacks*.
13. They brought with them *ethnic* traditions.
14. They were *tolerant* of each other.
15. They had different *beliefs*.
16. People of different beliefs are *married* to each other.
17. They respect people whose background is *different*.
18. It is necessary to settle *differences*.
19. Not everyone was born under equal *circumstances*.
20. Everyone has the right to the *pursuit* of happiness.
21. The Americans are a *proud* people.
22. To live in a democracy means to suffer *sacrifices*.
23. People must *adjust* to a situation.
24. They are tough but *charitable*.
25. The *newcomers* want to be called "Americans."

B. Fill in the blanks with words from the narrative. Each space may be filled by a word or phrase. Do not refer back to the narrative. Where possible, use variations of the missing words. Read aloud.

Many people _____ wished to _____ a new life _____ across the seven _____ . They sailed to the _____ of America. The _____ jets _____ the immigrants. They are _____ by some _____ goals. Many come in _____ of _____ to worship _____ they find here. For those _____ come, the United States of America is _____ the land of _____ .

Some people _____ on land _____ is fertile. They are _____ by the great _____ that span the land. A _____ could travel three thousand _____ across this _____ and no one _____ questions. There are no _____ to cross, no _____ to present.

The same human _____ which accompanied them to the _____ became great _____ . People of _____ national _____ settled _____ to each _____ . They were _____ of each other's _____ beliefs. But they refused to _____ their children to _____ or intermarry.

But as the _____ increases, people come to _____ closer _____ . They _____ to _____ differences, and accept _____ . They _____ people _____ backgrounds are _____ their own.

The Americans are a _____ people. They are proud of their _____ . They remember the _____ and the _____ of the _____ . They know _____ to live in a _____ means to _____ many _____ . The Americans are _____ to _____ .

Their president _____ authority they _____ will _____ them. The Americans _____ to _____ their leadership in _____ elections.

The Americans _____ are _____ working. But they are _____ . They are always _____ to _____ their fellow _____ . This is the _____ why so many come to this _____ called the _____ of _____ .

V. Grammar and Syntax   (Points of Interest)

Relative Clauses Modifying Nouns. Two sentences may be combined when a noun in one sentence is identical with a noun in a second sentence. In such cases, a RELATIVE PRONOUN such as *who, whom, which, whose,* etc., will replace the noun in the second sentence when the two sentences are joined.

A.   **Relative Pronoun as Subject.** In the following examples, the relative pronouns *who* (referring to persons), *which* (referring to things), or *that* (referring to persons or things) replace the noun (subject) in the second sentence.

   1. Many people wished to seek a new life.
   2. *People* sailed across the seven seas.
      (who)

   3. Many people *who* wished to seek a new life sailed across the seven seas.

1. Jets transported the immigrants.
2. *The immigrants* came from almost every country.
    (who)

3. Jets transported the immigrants *who* came from almost every country.

1. Some people settle on land.
2. *The land* is very fertile.
    (that)

3. Some people settle on land *that* is very fertile.

B.   Relative Pronoun as **Object**. In the following examples, the relative pronouns *whom, which,* or *that* replace the object of the second sentence.

1. The newcomers are happy with the people.
2. They meet *the people* in their new homeland.
    (whom)

3. The newcomers are happy with the people *whom* they meet in their new homeland.

1. Many come in search of freedom to worship.
2. They find *freedom to worship* here.
    (that)

3. Many come in search of freedom to worship *that* they find here.

1. Some people look for land to settle on.
2. They find *fertile land* to settle on.
    (which)

3. Some people look for fertile land *which* they can settle on.

Note: In conversation, the RELATIVE PRONOUN as OBJECT is often omitted. See third example on the following page.

The people *whom* they met   . . . (formal)
The people *that* they met   . . . (informal)
The people they met   . . . (conversational)

— — — — — — — — — — — — — — — — — — —

C. **Relative Pronoun** as **Modifier** of **Noun.** In the following examples, the relative pronoun *whose* replaces the possessive form of a noun.

1. They respect people.
2. The *people's* background is unlike their own.
   (whose)

3. They respect people *whose* background is unlike their own.

1. The president will lead them.
2. They respect the *leader's* authority.
   (whose)

3. The president *whose* authority they respect will lead them.

VI. *Word Recognition*

A. Circle the word in Column II most *like* the word in Column I, and circle the word or phrase in Column II most *unlike* the word in Column I. This oral identification of words ought to be timed.

COLUMN I	COLUMN II		COLUMN III	
1. **awe**	a.	advice	a.	irreverence
	b.	equality	b.	inequality
	c.	reverence	c.	deterrent
2. **charitable**	a.	soft	a.	selfish
	b.	benevolent	b.	tough
	c.	trustworthy	c.	able to take adversity

3. **endeavor**
   a. dominate
   b. work
   c. advise

   a. give up
   b. be idle
   c. conflict

4. **establish**
   a. organize
   b. seek
   c. settle

   a. move on
   b. find
   c. break up

5. **fertile**
   a. complete
   b. private
   c. fruitful

   a. arid
   b. careless
   c. public

6. **inalienable**
   a. unreliable
   b. guilty
   c. indisputable

   a. disputable
   b. innocent
   c. untrustworthy

7. **recently**
   a. beyond
   b. lately
   c. farther

   a. near
   b. long ago
   c. reasonable

8. **respect**
   a. regard
   b. divorce
   c. confuse

   a. dissimilarity
   b. difference
   c. abuse

9. **setback**
   a. obstacle
   b. border
   c. belief

   a. interior
   b. advancement
   c. disbelief

10. **shore**
   a. sail
   b. travel
   c. coastline

   a. ocean
   b. space
   c. span

B. In the space on the left write the word(s) that best fit the expression in **bold print**. Make other necessary changes. Read aloud.

_____ 1. People **traveled by boat.**

_____ 2. **Lately,** they come by jet.

_____ 3. They seek freedom to **pray.**

_____ 4. Some **establish themselves** on land.

_____ 5. The land is **fruitful.**

_____ 6. There are no **boundaries.**

_____ 7. There were some **obstacles.**

_____ 8. People remember their **cultural** background.

_____ 9. Many don't **fraternize** with one another.

_____ 10. They make the best of the **situation.**

_____ 11. The Americans are **self-satisfied.**

_____ 12. They remember their **tradition.**

_____ 13. Much is **surrendered** in democracy.

_____ 14. The Americans **adapt** well.

_____ 15. The Americans are **firm.**

_____ 16. But they are **benevolent.**

VII. *Concept Recognition*

Fill in the word (phrase) most fitting to express the CONCEPT of the sentence according to the narrative. Read the completed sentence aloud.

A. People sailed to the United States of America to seek _____ .

1. counsel
2. a new life
3. their relatives
4. the seven seas

B. They were bound by _____ .

1. some common goals
2. the fastest jets
3. every country
4. different nationalities

C. They were awed by _____ .

1. the land
2. the small cities
3. the great distances
4. the fertile land

D. A person could travel across the three thousand miles, and there were

_____ .

1. no boundaries
2. passports to cross
3. happy people
4. unhappy people

E.   Even though the people were happy, there were_____ .

    1. questions   2. some setbacks
    3. answers   4. similar backgrounds

F.   People of similar national backgrounds settled _____ .

    1. on land   2. in the cities
    3. close to each other   4. far from each other

G.   Some people settled close to each other because they were of _____ national backgrounds.

    1. similar   2. different
    3. profound   4. least

H.   They refused to allow their children to associate because they_____ .

    1. were Americans   2. had different beliefs
    3. were immigrants   4. were tolerant

I.   People live closer together when _____ .

    1. the population increases 2. their backgrounds are different
    3. their differences are   4. they like their neighbors
       greater

J.   Everyone has the right to_____ .

    1. live in the United States 2. live on land
    3. live in the city   4. the pursuit of happiness

K.   In a democracy much is _____ .

    1. done   2. needed
    3. forgotten   4. sacrificed

L.   The Americans are proud, but they are also_____ .

    1. leaders   2. charitable
    3. elected   4. ready

M.   Because they are used to changes, the Americans know how to _____ .

    1. be kind   2. make the best of a situation
    3. elect their president   4. work hard

VIII. *Telling the Meaning*

A. Place a check mark (✓) in front of the word in COLUMN II that best fits the MEANING of the word in COLUMN I. Read aloud a complete sentence using this word.

COLUMN I   COLUMN II

1. **adjust**
                                                  _____ a. surrender
    _____ b. sacrifice
    _____ c. adapt

2. **belief**
    _____ a. faith
    _____ b. fortune
    _____ c. disbelief

3. **border**
    _____ a. interior
    _____ b. boundary
    _____ c. land

4. **ethnic**
    _____ a. biased
    _____ b. national
    _____ c. cultural

5. **fortune**
    _____ a. poverty
    _____ b. income
    _____ c. wealth

6. **fruitful**
    _____ a. orderly
    _____ b. fertile
    _____ c. arid

7. **immigrant**
    _____ a. settler
    _____ b. emigrant
    _____ c. traveler

8. **obstacle**
    _____ a. span
    _____ b. setback
    _____ c. advancement

9. **ocean**
    _____ a. shore
    _____ b. coastline
    _____ c. ground

10. **proud**   _____ a.   tough
                           _____ b.   ashamed
                           _____ c.   charitable

11. **reverence**   _____ a.   awe
                           _____ b.   prayer
                           _____ c.   irreverence

12. **settle**   _____ a.   move on
                           _____ b.   establish oneself
                           _____ c.   advance

13. **tolerant**   _____ a.   intolerant
                           _____ b.   understanding
                           _____ c.   religious

14. **underneath**   _____ a.   profound
                           _____ b.   beneath
                           _____ c.   shallow

15. **work**   _____ a.   respect
                           _____ b.   endeavor
                           _____ c.   pursuit

16. **worship**   _____ a.   blaspheme
                           _____ b.   pray
                           _____ c.   sail

B. Select one of the three (3) words (phrases) that best fulfills the MEANING of the sentence according to the narrative. Insert the word in the blank space. Read the completed sentence aloud.

1. The immigrants came to the United States to seek_____ .
   a. a new life   b. poverty   c. obstacles

2. The immigrants fly on jets to arrive_____ .
   a. faster   b. in the city   c. on land

3. There are many different nationalities, but there are some_____ .
   a. good people   b. poor immigrants   c. common goals

4. The immigrants settle on land because they know it is _____ .
   a. arid   b. fertile   c. vast

5. The people are awed by the great _____ that _____ the land.
   a. distances, span   b. homes, grow   c. opportunity, travels

6. The people can travel far because there are no _____ to cross.
   a. borders   b. questions   c. passports

7. There were some _____ in the New World.
   a. newcomers   b. obstacles   c. elements

8. The immigrants settled close to each other because of _____ national backgrounds.
   a. different   b. similar   c. prejudiced

9. The newcomers believed that their children should stay in their own _____ group.
   a. age   b. ethnic   c. intelligence

10. They would not allow their children to _____ outside their group, or to
    a. play, study   b. associate, intermarry   c. settle, travel

11. People come to live closer together because _____.
    a. they like each other   b. they like to travel   c. population increases

12. Because people live closer together, they learn to _____.
    a. worship together   b. play together   c. tolerate differences

13. They find it necessary to _____ their _____ peacefully.
    a. settle, differences   b. play, games   c. plan, vacations

14. People respect each other because everyone has the right to the _____.
    a. equal circumstances   b. pursuit of happiness   c. same fortune

15. Even though this is a democracy, there are many _____ to be made.
    a. sacrifices   b. fortunes   c. situations

16. In changing situations, people must get used to _____.
    a. fortunes   b. adjustments   c. bad leadership

17. When a leader proves untrustworthy, the Americans _____ .
    a. will not keep him   b. will vote for him c. will elect him

18. The Americans are tough and hard-working, but they don't forget to

    _____ .

    a. play   b. help their   c. make a fortune
                                  fellowman

IX.   Comprehension   [Exercises]

A.   Place a check mark (✓) in front of the correct response to each of the
     statements according to the narrative. Read the completed sentence aloud.

     1. Many people sailed across the seas

        _____ a. for no reason at all.
        _____ b. to seek a new life.
        _____ c. to seek common friends.

     2. The immigrants are bound by

        _____ a. common religion.
        _____ b. common social classes.
        _____ c. common goals.

     3. For most newcomers, America is

        _____ a. the land of opportunity.
        _____ b. the land to worship.
        _____ c. the land of common goals.

     4. Some people settle on land because it is

        _____ a. very fertile.
        _____ b. very vast.
        _____ c. very arid.

     5. The newcomers are awed by the

        _____ a. many cities.
        _____ b. many people.
        _____ c. great distances.

6. One could travel three thousand miles across this country and

_____ a. there are no borders.
_____ b. there are no people.
_____ c. there are no fortunes.

7. Though the people are happy, there are

_____ a. many children.
_____ b. many cities.
_____ c. some setbacks.

8. People of similar national backgrounds settled

_____ a. with the other groups.
_____ b. on land.
_____ c. close to each other.

9. Though they were different, they

_____ a. learned to tolerate each other.
_____ b. learned to play with each other.
_____ c. refused to talk to each other.

10. Because of ethnic differences they refused to

_____ a. settle on land.
_____ b. play games.
_____ c. allow their children to intermarry.

11. People came to live closer together because

_____ a. population increased.
_____ b. they liked each other.
_____ c. they liked their children.

12. People are not born under equal circumstances, but

_____ a. they have equal rights.
_____ b. they can emigrate.
_____ c. they can live on land.

13. To live in a democracy means to

_____ a. live free and easy.
_____ b. suffer many sacrifices.
_____ c. change.

14. People make the best of a situation when

    ____ a. they are equal.
    ____ b. they live together.
    ____ c. they adjust to changes.

15. Though the Americans are tough, they

    ____ a. help others.
    ____ b. don't like the immigrants.
    ____ c. don't help others.

B. Below there are three (3) different thoughts expressed in each of the exercises. Assign the proper sequence (order) of THOUGHT, according to the narrative, by numbering 1 to 3. Read aloud.

1. a. who wished to seek a new life   _____
   b. many people   _____
   c. sailed across the seven seas   _____

2. a. transport the immigrants   _____
   b. to the United States   _____
   c. the fastest jets   _____

3. a. of freedom to worship   _____
   b. many come in search   _____
   c. that they find here   _____

4. a. the United States of America is   _____
   b. for those who come   _____
   c. still the land of opportunity   _____

5. a. in big and small cities   _____
   b. of this vast land   _____
   c. some people seek a home   _____

6. a. that span the land   _____
   b. they are awed   _____
   c. by the great distances   _____

7. a. with the people whom   _____
   b. they met in their new homeland   _____
   c. the newcomers were happy   _____

8. a. without some setbacks   ———————
   b. was not altogether   ———————
   c. but this happiness   ———————

9. a. national backgrounds   ———————
   b. people of similar   ———————
   c. settled close to each other   ———————

10. a. each other's religious beliefs   ———————
    b. for the most part,   ———————
    c. they were tolerant of   ———————

11. a. increases, people come   ———————
    b. to live closer together   ———————
    c. but as the population   ———————

12. a. differences, and   ———————
    b. they learn to tolerate   ———————
    c. accept changes   ———————

13. a. not everyone   ———————
    b. under equal circumstances   ———————
    c. was born   ———————

14. a. but every individual   ———————
    b. pursuit of his own happiness   ———————
    c. has the right to the   ———————

15. a. live in a democracy means   ———————
    b. they know that to   ———————
    c. to suffer many sacrifices   ———————

16. a. the best of a situation, and   ———————
    b. they know how to make   ———————
    c. they adjust easily to changes   ———————

17. a. will lead them   ———————
    b. their president whose   ———————
    c. authority they respect   ———————

18. a. in free elections   ———————
    b. to elect their leadership   ———————
    c. the Americans vote   ———————

19. a. they are   _____
  b. underneath that toughness _____
  c. charitable   _____

20. a. ready to help   _____
  b. they are always   _____
  c. their fellow man   _____

21. a. so many come to this land   _____
  b. this is the reason why   _____
  c. called the United States of America _____

22. a. to be called   _____
  b. they, too, want   _____
  c. Americans   _____

C. There are some statements listed below about the narrative. Write **T** for **True** in front of each statement that you think is true. Write **F** for **False** if the statement is not true. Read aloud.

_____ 1. All people come to the United States to make a fortune.

_____ 2. They come from almost every country.

_____ 3. People of different nationalities come to the United States.

_____ 4. The immigrants have one common goal.

_____ 5. America is the land of opportunity for many.

_____ 6. The land in the United States is very fertile.

_____ 7. The people are awed by the great fortune.

_____ 8. They cannot travel far because of borders.

_____ 9. The immigrants must carry passports to travel in the United States.

_____ 10. The newcomers are happy with the people they meet.

_____ 11. Their happiness has some setbacks .

_____ 12. The immigrants brought with them some prejudices.

_____ 13. People of different national backgrounds settle close to each other.

_____ 14. For the most part, they are tolerant of each other.

_____ 15. But the immigrants refuse to allow their children to intermarry.

_____ 16. People come to live closer together when population increases.

_____ 17. They do not respect people who are unlike their own.

_____ 18. They settle their differences peacefully.

_____ 19. Everyone was born under equal circumstances.

_____ 20. Everyone has the right to the pursuit of his happiness.

_____ 21. The Americans are proud people.

_____ 22. To live in a democracy means to suffer sacrifices.

_____ 23. The Americans are not used to changes.

_____ 24. They make the best of a situation.

_____ 25. A respected leader will lead them.

_____ 26. There are free elections.

_____ 27. People will not vote for an untrustworthy leader.

_____ 28. The Americans are hard working.

_____ 29. They are tough, but charitable.

_____ 30. The Americans help their fellow man.

X. Composition and Discussion

A.   In COLUMN I are the beginnings of sentences. In COLUMN II are the completions to sentences of COLUMN I. Select the completion best fitting each sentence in COLUMN I according to the narrative. Read the completed sentences orally. Compose new sentences orally and discuss the narrative.

COLUMN I

1. Many people sailed . . . .
2. The fastest jets . . . .
3. Some look for food, ...
4. Some people settle on land . . . . .
5. They are awed by the . . . .
6. There are no borders to cross, . . .
7. This happiness was not altogether .
8. They brought with them . . . .
9. People of similar backgrounds . . .

COLUMN II

a. under equal circumstances.
b. used to changes.
c. hard-working and tough.
d. to help their fellow man.
e. others for fortune.
f. and accept changes.
g. of each other's beliefs.
h. no passports to present.
i. across the seven seas.

10. They were tolerant . . . .   j. that is very fertile.
11. As the population increases . . . . .   k. great distances that span the land.
12. They learn to tolerate differences .   l. people come to live closer together.
13. Not everyone was born . . . .   m. settled close to each other.
14. The Americans are . . . .   n. well-established prejudices.
15. The American people are . . . .   o. without some setbacks.
16. They are always ready . . . .   p. transport the immigrants.

B. 1. Tell us about your most memorable trip.
2. Why did you travel?
3. Describe the circumstances in your country.
4. Tell us what you think about the people you met.
5. Tell us how you adjusted to the changes.
6. Tell us what you think about helping others.

C.   Tell us what you think when I say:

immigrant — the United States of America — prejudice — land of opportunity — tradition — nationality — work — tough — kind — equal rights — revolution — elections

D.   Read the poem aloud. Answer orally the questions listed following the poem.

Poverty[1]   [1] being poor

How poor, indeed, is he who
has the means[2] *to make*   [2] way
his dreams come true
in time to hear a wish!

Can you compare the riches[3]   [3] wealth
of forgotten fable-lands
to dreams that slowly
become reality?

How poor, indeed, is he who
knows no peace of spirit,[4] *nor*   [4] mind
the blessing of a wish that he
can shout[5] *at time and space. .*   [5] yell

Can he compare the
riseches of his wasted[6] days
to dreams that slowly
come to be?

[6] spent in vain

1. Read orally the stanzas where you find related words to the title of the poem.
2. Read orally the stanzas where you find antonyms of the title.
3. Explain the meaning of the first stanza. Discuss it in class.
4. What is the meaning of the first two lines of the third stanza? Discuss it in class.
5. Does the poem express poverty or wealth, or both? Discuss it in class.

E. Describe what you see in the picture below.

* * * * * *

Chapter Ten

News Gazette

**Office collects lost articles
of careless college students**

> **Words to remember:**
> *this, that, these, those*
>
> RELATIVE PRONOUN
> *whom, which, that*
>
> ADVERB—ADVERBIAL PHRASE
> *where — when*

I. Narrative

The person to whom he was speaking was a young college freshman. Mr. Ungerer, the director of student activities, was serious. "I can't understand why most of the students leave things lying around." He pointed in the direction of a large box. "Do you see that box? It's full of lost and found articles." The lost and found office on the first floor of the Administration Building has collected many lost items. This is the place where they are kept.

Mr. Ungerer said students are advised to put identifying marks on their books. "They ought to put the marks where you can see them. This way items would be returned to the owner quickly."

"Some students say that if they put their names on their books it will lower the resale value of their books," he added. "But that's ridiculous!"

Another factor leading to lost items is that students trust everyone. "Talk does little to warn the students," Ungerer continued. "We carry our discussions to a point where a decision must be made. The students must make this decision. They must care for their possessions." Mr. Ungerer gave some further advice. If a student loses an item, the student should check the area where the item was lost. If the item is gone, check with the lost and found office. Keep checking with the lost and found office. Ungerer said he has hundreds of dollars worth of books and clothing that have never been claimed.

This reporter is glad she was there at the time Ungerer offered his advice. Now we pass it on to you, the student, for what it may be worth. Take advantage of it!

The Letter

September 21, 1973

Dear David:

Because of some urgent work that I did not anticipate, I had to delay this letter. I know you've been waiting impatiently for the manuscript which I promised to send. It is almost finished now. The person to whom I'll send it is Bruce. You've instructed me to forward it to him. I understand the publication date toward which we aim is the fifteenth of January.

I want you to know that it was great fun to write this book. I can only hope that the students will enjoy it equally. If you have any suggestions to make concerning the manuscript, please feel free to do so.

The other night we went to the restaurant where we ate with you. Do you remember the place? "Alonso's." Of course, our conversation was about how much you've enjoyed eating there. The restaurant was filled to capacity. You were there with us at the time when the place was only recently opened. The crowds were smaller then. It's nothing important. I only wanted you to know that we always remember you.

Take good care. Give my regards to Weldon, Bruce, and all our friends. The very best to you from the family. Keep in touch.

With kindest regards.

Cordially,

Bill

* * *

II. *Words in Context   [Pictographs]*

Below are some of the words used in the news article and the letter. Where possible, each word has a [synonym], or it is defined as used in the story. Where possible, an (*antonym*) is also given. Make up sentences about the pictographs choosing the words you need. Read aloud.

Example: [serious] = They spoke in earnest.

A.

Drawing of paragraph A

serious [earnest] (*funny*); around [about]; full [filled] (*empty*); article [thing]; collect [gather] (*distribute*); mark [sign]; value [worth] (*uselessness*); ridiculous [not sensible] (*serious*); factor [element]; decision [determination] (*indecision*); possession [belonging]; claim [identify as one's own] (*disclaim*)

B.

Drawing of paragraph B

urgent [**important**] (*unimportant*); impatient [**restless**] (*patient*); manuscript [**book**]; promise [**pledge**]; forward [**send**] (*keep*); publication date
[**date the finished book is offered to the public**]

III. *Structures   [Phrases]*

Below are some PHRASES taken from the news article and the letter.
Make complete sentences and read them aloud.

OFFICE COLLECTS LOST ARTICLES

A. of   —   careless   —   students

B.	person	—	to	—	whom
C.	of	—	student	—	activities
D.	things	—	lying	—	around
E.	direction	—	in	—	which
F.	a	—	large	—	box
G.	of	—	lost	—	and found
H.	the	—	first	—	floor
I.	of	—	the	—	Administration
J.	many	—	lost	—	items
K.	the	—	place	—	where
L.	identifying	—	marks		
M.	marks	—	where		
N.	to	—	the	—	owner
O.	on	—	their	—	books
P.	the	—	resale	—	value
Q.	of	—	their	—	books
R.	to	—	lost	—	items
S.	a	—	point	—	where
T.	for	—	their	—	possessions
U.	the	—	area	—	where
V.	worth	—	of	—	books
W.	on	—	to	—	you

THE LETTER

A.	because	—	of	—	work
B.	delay	—	this	—	letter
C.	for	—	the	—	manuscript
D.	the	—	person	—	to whom
E.	the	—	publication	—	date
F.	toward	—	which		
G.	great	—	fun		
H.	concerning	—	the	—	manuscript
I.	the	—	restaurant	—	where
J.	a	—	time	—	when
K.	only	—	recently		
L.	the	—	crowds	—	smaller
M.	all	—	our	—	friends
N.	very	—	best	—	to you
O.	kindest	—	regards		

IV. *Sentences*

A. Read the following sentences aloud. Repeat, substituting where possible, the synonym of the word in *italics*.

Example: There were items lying *around*.
There were items lying *about*.

1. The director was *serious*.
2. He *pointed* to a large box.
3. The box was full of lost and found *articles*.
4. The office has *collected* many items.
5. Put your *marks* where you can see them.
6. It will lower the resale *value*.
7. Talk does little to *warn* students.
8. A *decision* must be made.
9. They must care for their *possessions*.
10. Mr. Ungerer gave us some *advice*.
11. The student should check the *area*.
12. We *pass it on* to you.
13. I did not anticipate *urgent* work.
14. You've been waiting *impatiently*.
15. The person to whom I'll send the *manuscript* is Bruce.
16. You've instructed me to *forward* it to him.
17. The students will enjoy it *equally*.
18. Feel free to make *suggestions*.
19. We *conversed* about you.
20. The restaurant was *filled* to *capacity*.
21. The place was only *recently* opened.

B. Fill in the blanks with words from the readings. Each space may be filled by a word or phrase. Do not refer back to the narrative. Where possible, use variations of the missing words. Read aloud.

The person to _____ he was speaking was a _____college freshman. The _____ of _____ activities was _____ . He pointed in the direction of a large _____ . This is the place _____ they are _____.

Mr. Ungerer, director of student _____ , said students are _____ to put _____ marks on their _____ . "They ought to _____ the marks _____ you can _____ them."

Students _____ everyone. "We carry our_____ to a point _____ a decision must be _____. The students must _____ this _____ . They must _____ for their _____ ."

The students should_____ the area_____the item was _____. Keep _____ with the_____ and _____ office.

This reporter is_____ she was_____ at the _____Ungerer_____his _____. Now we_____ it on to _____. Take _____!

_____David:

Because of_____ urgent work _____ I did not_____ , I had to _____ this_____. I know you've been_____ impatiently for the_____which I promised to _____ . It is _____ finished now. The person to _____ I'll send it is Bruce. I understand, the publication _____ toward _____ we aim is the fifteenth of_____ .

It was great_____ to write this_____ . I can only_____ that the _____ will _____ it_____ .

The other_____ we went to the restaurant_____we ate with you. Do you _____ the place? I know, you've _____ eating there. The restaurant was _____ to_____. I only wanted you to _____that we always _____ you.

Take _____ care. Give my_____ to Weldon, Bruce, and all our_____ . The very_____ to you from the _____ . Keep in _____.

                                                 With _____ regards,

V.   Grammar and Syntax   *(Points of Interest)*

A.   The **Relative Pronouns** *whom, which,* or *that* may replace the object of the preposition.

   1. The *person* is a young college freshman.
   2. He was speaking to *this person.*
            (whom)

   3. The person / to *whom* he was speaking / was a young college freshman.

   1. There was a *large box.*
   2. He pointed in *the direction* of a large box.
        (which)

   3. The direction / in *which* he pointed / was a large box.

NOTE: In informal speech *that* is often substituted for *which.* The preposition stands after the verb or object. The **relative pronoun** is often omitted in conversation.

The person (*that*) he was talking to was a young college freshman.

In the direction (*that*) he pointed to was a large box.

— — — — — — — — — — — — — — — — — — — —

B.   The **Relative Pronoun** *where* often replace an **adverb** or **adverbial phrase** indicating location.

1. This is the *place.*
2. They are kept *in this place.*
        *(***where***)*
          ↓
3. This is the place *where* they are kept.

1. We carry our discussions to a point.
2. *At this point* a decision must be made.
     (where)⟶
3. We carry our discussions to a point *where* a decision must be made.

1. The student should check the area.
2. The item was lost *in this area.*
        (where)
3. The student should check the area *where* the item was lost.

Note: An **adverb** or **adverbial phrase** may be replaced by the **relative pronoun** *when.*

1. You were there with us at the time.
2. The place was opened *at that time.*
        (when)
3. You were there with us at the time *when* the place was opened.

VI.   *Word Recognition*

A.   Circle the word(s) in Column II most *like* that in Column I, and circle the word(s) in Column III most *unlike* the word in Column I. This oral identification of words ought to be timed.

COLUMN I	COLUMN II		COLUMN III	
1. **claim**	a.	notice	a.	disclaim
	b.	identify as one's own	b.	neglect
	c.	move	c.	rest
2. **collect**	a.	accept	a.	carry
	b.	gather	b.	sell
	c.	attend	c.	distribute
3. **full**	a.	filled	a.	idle
	b.	easy	b.	late
	c.	wary	c.	empty
4. **impatient**	a.	perfect	a.	patient
	b.	restless	b.	spacious
	c.	private	c.	public
5. **ridiculous**	a.	insignificant	a.	innocent
	b.	not sensible	b.	funny
	c.	easy-going	c.	serious
6. **serious**	a.	good	a.	lazy
	b.	earnest	b.	unable
	c.	eager	c.	funny
7. **urgent**	a.	important	a.	devious
	b.	clamorous	b.	simple
	c.	public	c.	unimportant
8. **value**	a.	worth	a.	habit
	b.	endeavor	b.	idleness
	c.	factor	c.	uselessness

B. In the space on the left write the word(s) that would best fit the expression in **bold print**. Make other necessary changes. Read aloud.

_____ 1. The director was **earnest**.

_____ 2. The students leave things lying **about**.

_____ 3. There are many lost **items**.

_____ 4. We **gather** the items here.

_____ 5. The students must **sign** their books.

_____ 6. One must value one's **possessions**.

_____ 7. You should **claim** the articles.

_____ 8. The matter is **pressing**.

_____ 9. I know you are **impatient**.

_____ 10. I'll **send** it, as I promised.

VII. *Concept Recognition*

Fill in the most appropriate word (phrase) to express the CONCEPT of the sentence according to the readings. Read the completed sentence aloud.

A. The director was speaking to a student about _____ .

   1. lost items   2. activities
   3. lying around   4. a large box

B. The director pointed to a box which was full of _____ articles.

   1. student activities   2. lost and found
   3. college freshmen   4. persons

C. He advised students to mark their books so that they would be _____ to the owner quickly.

   1. put   2. kept
   3. returned   4. valued

D. Students don't put marks in their books because this would _____ .

   1. be returned   2. be kept
   3. mark the book   4. lower the resale value

E. Talk does little to warn students because they _____ .

   1. trust everybody   2. have many books
   3. don't care   4. are the owners

F.   The director can give advice, but the students must make the _____ .

   1. possession   2. decision
   3. loss   4. warning

G.   Students don't care for their lost items enough to _____ with the office.

   1. decide   2. trust
   3. check   4. advise

H.   Many items remain in the lost and found office _____ .

   1. claimed   2. unclaimed
   3. checked   4. dated

I.   The reporter was glad to talk to the director because she could _____ the other students about it.

   1. tell   2. claim
   3. take advantage   4. point

VIII.   *Telling the Meaning*

A.   Place a check mark (✓) in front of the word in Column II that best fits the MEANING of the word in Column I. Read aloud a complete sentence using this word.

COLUMN I   COLUMN II

1. **about**   _____ a.   empty
                            _____ b.   around
                            _____ c.   earnest

2. **claim**   _____ a.   disclaim
                            _____ b.   possess
                            _____ c.   identify as one's own

3. **comic**   _____ a.   incriminating
                            _____ b.   serious
                            _____ c.   ridiculous

4. **decision**   _____ a.   determination
                            _____ b.   indecision
                            _____ c.   celebration

5. **declaration**
   - _____ a. trust
   - _____ b. publication
   - _____ c. secrecy

6. **demand**
   - _____ a. disclaim
   - _____ b. claim
   - _____ c. detain

7. **determination**
   - _____ a. indecision
   - _____ b. decision
   - _____ c. distrust

8. **earnest**
   - _____ a. serious
   - _____ b. funny
   - _____ c. responsible

9. **gather**
   - _____ a. collect
   - _____ b. gain
   - _____ c. distribute

10. **important**
   - _____ a. secure
   - _____ b. urgent
   - _____ c. unimportant

11. **possession**
   - _____ a. promise
   - _____ b. belonging
   - _____ c. pledge

12. **restless**
   - _____ a. impatient
   - _____ b. patient
   - _____ c. satisfied

13. **send**
   - _____ a. forward
   - _____ b. break up
   - _____ c. keep

14. **worth**
   - _____ a. uselessness
   - _____ b. value
   - _____ c. gain

B. Select one of the three (3) words (phrases) that best fulfills the MEANING of the sentence according to the readings. Insert the word in the blank space. Read the completed sentence aloud.

1. The director spoke to a _____ college freshman.
   a. young   b. person   c. friendly

2. The director was _____ when he spoke.
   a. happy   b. amicable   c. serious

3. He pointed to a box full of _____ .
   a. books   b. lost and found   c. marks
                               articles

4. The lost and found office _____ items.
   a. collects   b. loses   c. sends

5. Students lose articles because they don't put _____ in them.
   a. money   b. marks   c. books

6. They ought to put the marks where you could _____ them.
   a. keep   b. lower   c. see

7. It lowers the resale value of books when students write their _____
   on them.
   a. story   b. marks   . c. names

8. Many items are lost because the students _____ everybody.
   a. see   b. like   c. trust

9. Only the students can make a _____ to _____ for their possessions.
   a. decision, care   b. discussion, talk   c. point, carry

10. There are always many items in the office which the students don't
    _____ .
    a. claim   b. see   c. lose

IX.   *Comprehension   [Exercises]*

A.   Place a check mark (✓) in front of the correct answer to each of the
questions according to the readings. Read the complete reply aloud.

1. To whom was the director speaking?

   _____ a. to a young college freshman
   _____ b. to a professor
   _____ c. to a lady

2. Why was the director serious?

_____ a. because he was talking
_____ b. because the student listened
_____ c. because students leave things lying around

3. What was in the box?

_____ a. it was full of lost and found articles
_____ b. it was full of books
_____ c. it was full of students

4. Where was the lost and found office?

_____ a. in the Administration Building
_____ b. at the house
_____ c. at the activities

5. Why should students put identifying marks on their books?

_____ a. to lower the resale value
_____ b. to have them returned quickly
_____ c. to trust everyone

6. Is it useful to warn students?

_____ a. yes, it is
_____ b. no, it's useless
_____ c. yes, it's useless

7. Who must make the decision?

_____ a. the director
_____ b. the college
_____ c. the student

8. Why are there so many items in the lost and found?

_____ a. because they keep everything there
_____ b. because students don't claim their possessions
_____ c. because students are glad

9. Why was Bill late in writing the letter to David?

_____ a. because of some urgent work
_____ b. because he forgot
_____ c. because he wrote to Bruce

10. What did Bill promise to do for David?

    ____a. he promised to write a letter
    ____b. he promised to send the manuscript
    ____c. he promised to call him

11. What is Bill asking for?

    ____a. he asks for the book
    ____b. he asks for suggestions
    ____c. he asks for more time

12. What can David expect soon?

    ____a. the restaurant
    ____b. the manuscript
    ____c. the call

13. In what way did Bill remember David?

    ____a. because Bill ate at the restaurant
    ____b. because Bill thought about David
    ____c. because Bill talked about David

14. What was it that Bill wanted David to know?

    ____a. that they ate at the restaurant
    ____b. that they thought about him
    ____c. that he would call David

B.   Below there are three (3) different thoughts expressed in each of the exercises. Assign the proper sequence (order) of THOUGHT, according to the readings, by numbering 1 to 3. Read aloud.

1. a. the person to whom   _____
   b. a young college freshman   _____
   c. he was speaking was   _____

2. a. of student activities   _____
   b. the director   _____
   c. was serious   _____

3. a. the direction of   _____
   b. a large box   _____
   c. he pointed in   _____

4. a. place where the articles   _____
   b. this is the   _____
   c. are kept   _____

5. a. they ought to put   _____
   b. you could see them   _____
   c. the marks where   _____

6. a. be returned to   _____
   b. this way items would   _____
   c. the owner quickly.   _____

7. a. lost items is that   _____
   b. another factor leading to   _____
   c. students trust everyone   _____

8. a. to a point where   _____
   b. a decision must be made   _____
   c. we carry our discussions   _____

9. a. check the area where   _____
   b. the student should   _____
   c. the item was lost   _____

10. a. check with the   _____
    b. lost and found office   _____
    c. if the item is gone,   _____

11. a. of dollars worth of books   _____
    b. Ungerer said he has hundreds   _____
    c. and clothing that have never been claimed   _____

12. a. this reporter is glad   _____
    b. Ungerer offered his advice   _____
    c. she was there at the time   _____

13. a. that I did not anticipate,   _____
    b. because of some urgent work   _____
    c. I had to delay this letter   _____

14. a. I'll send it   _____
    b. the person to whom   _____
    c. is Bruce   _____

15. a. toward which we aim   _____
    b. the publication date   _____
    c. is the fifteenth of January   _____

16. a. it was great fun   _____
    b. I want you to know that   _____
    c. to write this book   _____

17. a. that the students   _____
    b. will enjoy it equally   _____
    c. I can only hope   _____

18. a. to make concerning the manuscript,   _____
    b. if you have any suggestions   _____
    c. please feel free to do so   _____

19. a. to the restaurant   _____
    b. the other night we went   _____
    c. where we ate with you   _____

20. a. at the time when   _____
    b. you were with us   _____
    c. the place was only recently opened   _____

C. There are some statements listed below about the readings. Write **T** for **True** in front of each statement that you think is true. Write **F** for **False** if the statement is not true. Read aloud.

_____ 1. The director was speaking to his friend.

_____ 2. The director was serious.

_____ 3. Students leave things lying about.

_____ 4. There were many items in the box.

_____ 5. The lost and found office is at home.

_____ 6. Students put identifying marks on books.

_____ 7. Students trust nobody.

_____ 8. The decision must be made by the director.

_____ 9. Students should check with the lost and found.

_____ 10. Students come to claim their possessions.

_____ 11. The reporter is glad to listen to Ungerer.

_____ 12. Bill forgot to write to David.

_____ 13. David was waiting for the manuscript.

_____ 14. The manuscript is almost finished.

_____ 15. It was fun to write this book.

_____ 16. When Bill went to the restaurant, it was filled to capacity.

_____ 17. He talked about Dave.

X. Composition and Discussion

A. In Column I are the beginnings of sentences. In Column II are the completions to sentences of Column I. Select the completion best fitting each sentence in Column I according to the readings. Read the completed sentences orally. Compose new sentences orally and discuss.

COLUMN I	COLUMN II
1. He was speaking	a. where the articles are kept.
2. The director	b. of a large box.
3. He pointed in the direction	c. to write this book.
4. This is the place	d. that we remember you.
5. Talk does little	e. to a young college freshman.
6. The student must	f. was serious.
7. The student should check	g. this letter.
8. I had to delay	h. to warn students.
9. It was great fun	i. make this decision.
10. I only wanted you to know	j. the area where the item was lost.

B. 1. Tell us about your school activities.
2. Did you ever lose an item in school?
3. What did you do to reclaim the lost item?
4. Tell us about a letter you received.

C. Tell us what you think when I say:

lost and found — director of student activities — possessions — trust — decision — manuscript — crowds

D. Describe what you see in the picture below.

E. Read the poem aloud. Answer orally the questions listed following the poem.

Beautiful Soul

> Her face, I don't know
> where it was that he had
> seen it first, or did he
> see that which he sought[1]..?

[1]looked for

> What matters most, is
> that in her sweet
> expression he suddenly
> perceived[2] the goodness of humanity.

[2]saw

> And now, he shall no longer
> ask if there's some truth

to what they call the
"decent[3] kind"? For now,   [3] good

no measure of denial[4]   [4] saying "no"
can feign[5] destroy that   [5] assume
which his eyes perceived
across the way. . serene[6] and kind. . .   [6] peaceful

1. Identify the person speaking in the first stanza.
2. Identify the *relative pronouns* in this poem.
3. Does the title express the *main idea* of the poem?
4. Who is the "Beautiful Soul" of this poem? Discuss it in class.
5. What idea is expressed in the first stanza? Discuss this in class.
6. Does this poem appear sad or happy? Discuss it in class.

* * * * * *

Active Vocabulary

Words are listed in alphabetical order. The number preceding each word indicates the chapter where it was first used. The synonyms and antonyms are listed in the same manner as they were listed in the pictograph section.

CHAPTER	SYNONYM	ANTONYM
	A	
3 able	adequate	unable
4 abuse	maltreatment	care
3 accept	approve	reject
7 accident	mishap	purpose
7 accompany	escort	be alone
5 accomplish	achieve	give up
5 accountable	responsible	irresponsible
3 accusing	incriminating	
5 achieve	accomplish	fail
3 activity	action	inactivity
9 adjust	adapt	disturb
5 admonish	warn	
3 adopt	support	discard
2 afraid	frightened	unafraid
4 affectionate	tender	indifferent
8 afford	have the money for	
3 against	opposed	for
3 age	oldness	youth
4 agency	department	
5 ahead	foremost	behind
8 alien	immigrant	citizen
3 allow	permit	deny
1 also	too	
6 amazed	surprised	unamazed
6 ancestor	forebear	descendant
7 annual	yearly	
6 anticipation	expectation	

4	anxiety	fear	contentment
8	apologize	express regret	blame
2	appear	become visible	disappear
5	applause	acclamation	criticism
2	area	spot	
10	around	about	
1	arrive	come	depart
10	article	thing	
1	assemble	gather	scatter
9	associate	be friends	disassociate
7	assume	suppose	know
3	assure	promise	mislead
1	atmosphere	feeling	
4	attack	assault	aid
3	attend	be present	be absent
3	attentively	closely	negligently
5	attire	dress	undress
2	attorney	lawyer	
3	authority	power	subordination
3	avoid	shun	consent
5	aware	sensible	unaware
1	awe	reverence	irreverence

B

5	ballot	voting sheet	
6	banish	exile	shelter
2	be still	at rest	be active
2	before	prior to	after
1	begin	start	end
2	behave	obey	misbehave
9	belief	faith	disbelief
3	benefit	profit	lose
3	beyond	past	near
2	blanket	covering	
2	boat	vessel	
9	border	boundary	interior
3	break into	make illegal entry	
3	break out	begin	end
7	bridge	span	
2	bring	fetch	send
7	broad	wide	narrow
4	bruise	black and blue spot	
3	busing	transporting	

C

2	cabin	cottage	mansion
1	cafeteria	restaurant	
3	call on	visit	leave
2	camping	outing	
5	candidate	nominee	
2	canoe	boat	
4	capacity	ability	inability
7	careless	reckless	careful
2	carry	transport	
7	cave	underground chamber	
5	caution	warn	disregard
8	celebrate	observe festivities joyfully	
8	ceremony	ritual	
5	chance	opportunity	plan
5	change	alter	retain
9	charitable	benevolent	selfish
5	choice	many to pick from	limited selection
2	chore	task	
3	circumstance	occurrence	planned action
10	claim	identify as one's own	disclaim
1	class	group of students	
1	classmate	fellow student	
1	classroom	schoolroom	
3	clean	sanitary	dirty
6	clear	transparent	muddy
7	clearly	plainly	indistinctly
6	climb	ascend	descend
5	close	near	far
4	clumsy	awkward	graceful
10	collect	gather	distribute
6	colorless	lacking hue	colorful
1	come	arrive	go
6	community	society	disunity
4	complain	whine	approve
5	complete	total	incomplete
6	completely	entirely	not at all
2	concern	worry	unconcern
5	concerned	nervous	indifferent
3	confused	perplexed	orderly
5	conscious of	realistic	unrealistic
5	constant	always	seldom

3	constitutional	inherent	
5	continue	persist	cease
6	contrary	opposite	
3	contribute	donate	receive
2	control	balance	
3	convicted	found guilty	acquitted
5	convince	persuade	dissuade
5	cooperate	work together	oppose
5	council	planning body	
3	counsel	advise	deter
2	countryside	rural area	municipality
3	court	tribunal	
7	crawl	creep	run
6	creature	being	
2	cross	angry	happy
4	cruel	inhuman	gentle
4	cry	weep	laugh
7	crystalline	clear	unclear
6	curious	inquiring	indifferent
1	custom	fashion	

D

6	danger	peril	safety
7	dark	obscure	light
7	debris	rubble	
6	decide	determine	doubt
10	decision	determination	indecision
3	declare	affirm	stifle
7	deep	buried	shallow
3	deep	profound	shallow
1	delay	detain	hasten
3	deliberate	consider	
5	deliver	give	take
7	deputy	representative of law enforcement	
8	descent	origin	
2	desperately	hopelessly	hopefully
4	develop	grow	deteriorate
9	difference	dissimilarity	similarity
1	different	unlike	same
4	difficult	hard	easy
7	dig	excavate	bury
4	dirty	filthy	clean

2	discomfort	annoyance	contentment
7	discover	find	search
2	distance	remoteness	closeness
4	distrust	suspicion	trust
2	dive	plunge	
3	doubt	uncertainty	certainty
7	draft	current	
2	drag	pull	
5	dress	clothe	undress
2	drip	drop	
8	drop in	visit	depart
2	drown	sink	stay afloat
1	during	while	
5	duty	responsibility	freedom

E

1	eager	anxious	indifferent
7	echo	reverberation	
8	embarrass	perplex	relieve
8	embrace	hug	recoil
7	emerge	come out	go in
4	emotional	agitated	calm
6	enchanted	charmed	disenchanted
5	encourage	support	discourage
9	endeavor	work	idleness
5	entire	whole	partial
6	envious	jealous	satisfied
3	equal	same	unequal
4	especially	particularly	
8	establish	secure	break up
9	ethnic	cultural	
4	evident	clear	concealed
7	examine	investigate	answer
4	excited	enthusiastic	passive
2	exclaim	cry out	be silent
6	exist	live	die
6	explain	tell clearly	obscure
7	explore	investigate	ignore
4	extraordinary	remarkable	common

F

| 4 | face it | cope | avoid |
| 10 | factor | element | |

2	falls	waterfalls	
4	fear	dread	trust
4	feel	be concerned	ignore
9	fertile	fruitful	arid
5	fine	good	bad
5	finish	end	start
3	first	original	last
2	foam	froth	
6	foggy	misty	clear
3	follow	succeed	precede
8	following	next	previous
7	footing	support	
5	forceful	powerful	weak
9	fortune	wealth	poverty
6	forward	ahead	backward
10	forward	send	keep
4	foster	adopted	
7	fracture	break	mend
1	freeway	expressway	
1	friend		enemy
1	friendly	amicable	unfriendly
10	full	filled	empty
1	funny	strange	serious

G

1	get acquainted	meet	avoid
5	get ahead	progress	fall behind
1	glad	happy	sad
5	good behavior	good conduct	misbehavior
6	gossip	spread rumor	be discrete
4	gradual	step by step	sudden
6	greedy	avaricious	generous
2	groceries	food	
3	guard	sentry	
4	guess	suppose	be certain
3	guilty	at fault	innocent

H

5	habit	custom	
4	hallway	corridor	
7	halt	end	continue
5	hard	difficult to bear	easy-going
7	hasten	hurry	slow down

6	hate	detest	love
1	have	possess	lack
4	health	well-being	sickness
2	hear	listen	be deaf
8	heartily	sincerely	insincerely
2	help	assist	hinder
9	heritage	tradition	
2	hesitation	pause	haste
2	hilly	uneven terrain	flat land
2	hold on	grip	let go
7	hole	opening	
2	housewife	married woman in charge	career woman
		of a household	
6	huge	enormous	diminutive
4	hysterical	uncontrolled	calm

I

4	illness	sickness	health
7	immediately	at once	later
6	immense	enormous	tiny
9	immigrant	settler	emigrant
10	impatient	restless	patient
5	important	significant	insignificant
5	impress	affect	unimpress
8	impressive	imposing	unimpressive
8	improve	better	worsen
5	in front of	before	behind
9	inalienable	indisputable	disputable
3	income	salary	expenses
6	incorrigible	hopeless	hopeful
4	increase	grow	diminish
7	indicated	specified	unspecified
2	inexpensive	simple	ostentatious
4	infant	child	adult
6	inhabitant	occupant	
7	injury	damage	
3	innocence	lack of guilt	guilt
6	inquiry	question	statement
5	insist	maintain	yield
6	instead	in place of	
1	interesting	fascinating	boring
4	interference	coming between	not become involved
3	investigation	examination	
6	involved	confused, intricate	simple

J

7	joke	josh	be serious

K

3	kind	sympathetic	unkind
1	know	understand	be ignorant

L

7	labyrinth	maze	straight passage
4	lack	want	supply
2	late	delayed	early
5	lately	recently	long ago
1	laugh	chuckle	cry
2	law	rule	disorder
4	learn	be informed by	ignore
3	least	minimum	most
4	leave	depart	return
1	lesson	instruction	
5	let	allow	refuse
1	like	fond of	dislike
5	likewise	also	otherwise
1	listen	hear	ignore
2	living quarters	residence	
7	location	place	displacement
4	lock	confine	open
7	look forward to	anticipate	dread
2	lose	fail to keep	gain
6	loud	noisy	quiet
4	love	affection	hatred
3	low	small	high
7	lower	let down	raise
7	lucky	fortunate	unfortunate

M

5	maintain	keep	drop
2	make up	compensate	lack
4	manners	habitual or customary behavior	
10	manuscript	book	
1	many	a lot	few

1	map	chart	
10	mark	sign	
9	marry	wed	divorce
4	mature	grown up	immature
4	maybe	perhaps	impossible
3	mercy	pity	severity
8	minor	secondary	major
2	minute	moment	
4	mistreat	injure	care for
1	morning	early in the day	evening
3	most	greatest	least
6	mountain	large hill	valley
6	move	stir	rest
7	multiply	increase	decrease
4	mysterious	secret	obvious

N

1	name	title	
7	narrow	tight	wide
2	near	close	distant
4	neck	the part of man joining the head and body	
1	need	want	option
4	neglect	disregard	care
5	noise	clamor	stillness
5	notice	pay attention	neglect

O

8	occasion	opportunity	
2	occupation	line of work	leisure
3	offer	give	rescind
2	officer	official	
1	often	frequently	seldom
3	old	aged	young
4	open	show her feelings	withdrawn
5	opponent	adversary	friend
3	order	command	
3	orphanage	institution for children without parents	
4	overcome	conquer	succumb to
3	overcrowded	congested	spacious
2	own	possess	lack

P

1	part	section	whole
3	peer	equal	unequal
6	perfect	faultless	imperfect
3	personal	private	public
3	philanthropist	humanitarian	misanthrope
4	physical	bodily	emotional
2	picnic	outing	
1	place	locality	nowhere
3	place in custody	legal guardianship	
7	plan	arrange	chance
3	plea	request	
5	pledge	promise	refuse
3	point at	single out	
5	popular	favorite	unpopular
8	position	post	
10	possession	belonging	
7	precaution	care	carelessness
6	prejudice	bigotry	fairness
7	preparation	arrangement	unpreparedness
5	prepare	fix	
4	previous	prior	subsequent
4	problem	difficulty	solution
10	promise	pledge	
1	pronounce	articulate	
8	proper	appropriate	improper
9	proud	self-satisfied	ashamed
5	proudly	with pride	humbly
10	publication date	date the finished book is offered to the public	
7	pull	tow	push
4	pulse	heartbeat	
6	punish	chastise	reward
9	pursuit	striving	avoiding

Q

5	qualification	capability	inability
4	quick	fast	slow
4	quicken	accelerate	slow down
3	quickly	rapidly	slowly
3	quietly	silently	noisily

R

2	rapids	rushing water	
6	reach	arrive at	revert
3	reasonable	rational	unreasonable
9	recently	lately	long ago
3	recess	pause	
3	reconvene	meet again	recess
6	refuse	garbage	
4	refuse	decline	accept
1	relative	kinsman	stranger
1	relaxed	rested	tense
7	release	free	confine
4	reluctant	hesitant	willing
4	remain	continue	discontinue
5	remark	notice	disregard
2	rent	pay for the use of	
4	reply	answer	ignore
5	request	proposal	
8	required	necessary	unnecessary
7	rescue	save	endanger
8	residence	habitation	
9	respect	regard	abuse
2	respond	answer	ignore
5	response	reply	
2	rest	relax	work
4	return	come back	leave
3	reveal	disclose	cover up
2	ride	transport	
10	ridiculous	not sensible	serious
3	right	prerogative	
7	rock	large stone	
7	rope	cord	
4	rough	boisterous	gentle
2	run	flow	
4	run away	go away	stay

S

9	sacrifice	loss	profit
4	sad	depressed	gay
2	safe	out of danger	unsafe
9	sail	travel by boat	
8	save	redeem	lose
7	search	look for	discover

4	see	appear	conceal
3	seek	look for	find
5	select	pick	ignore, overlook
8	sell	trade for money	buy
5	sense	feel	ignore
3	sentence	judgment	acquittal
10	serious	earnest	funny
9	setback	obstacle	advancement
9	settle	establish oneself	move on
6	severely	harshly	leniently
6	shapeless	formless	formed
7	sheriff	county law enforcement officer	
8	shop	select	sell
2	short	small	long
1	show	point out	hide
6	side	edge	center
6	sight	seeing	blindness
8	sign	contract	
6	simple	uncomplicated	complicated
4	sincere	honest	feigned
7	skeleton	bony framework	
5	slow down	ease up	speed up
2	smile	grin	frown
4	social	public	personal
4	sofa	couch	
3	somebody	someone	nobody
3	something	anything	nothing
5	sound	seem	
9	span	extend	
4	speechless	without words	talkative
7	spelunking	cave exploring	
8	sponsor	support	
6	spot	place	
7	sprained	twisted	
6	spread	circulate	
8	stammer	stutter	
6	stand	tolerate	
1	stand up	get up	sit down
3	stern	severe	lenient
3	stolen	lifted	bought
2	stop	halt	go
5	strive	labor	loaf
5	stubborn	obstinate	docile

1	student	pupil	teacher
1	study	learn	
2	suddenly	abruptly	slowly
5	suggest	hint	declare
2	supermarket	grocery store	
2	supper	evening meal	breakfast
5	sure	certain	uncertain
6	surprise	astonish	forewarn
6	surround	encircle	
3	suspend	dismiss	
3	sustain	support	release
5	system	method	disorder
2	swim	stay afloat	sink

T

3	take over	assume control	lose
6	tall	high	short
1	teacher	instructor	student
3	team	group	individual
4	tension	anxiety	relaxation
4	terminal	fatal	curable
3	testify	witness	
1	think	reason	
3	thorough	complete	careless
6	throng	crowd	
7	tie	secure	untie
2	tip over	overturn	stay upright
2	toast	fry	
3	together	jointly	separately
9	tolerant	understanding	intolerant
6	top	summit	bottom
2	toss	fling	catch
9	tough	able to take adversity	soft
2	toward	in the direction of	away from
1	traffic jam	transportation stoppage	
1	travel	journey	stay home
2	tremble	shake	be still
3	trouble	difficulty	tranquility
8	trust	have faith	mistrust
6	try	attempt	abandon
2	turn back	turn around	go ahead
4	twinkle	sparkle	be expressionless

| 7 | twisting | curving | straight |
| 2 | typical | usual | unusual |

U

1	unable	incompetent	able
2	under	beneath	on top
9	underneath	beneath	above
6	unknown	unfamiliar	known
4	until	before	afterward
9	untrustworthy	unreliable	trustworthy
10	urgent	important	unimportant
4	useful	helpful	useless

V

1	vacation	holiday	work
6	vaguely	indefinitely	definitely
10	value	worth	uselessness
7	vast	immense	small
3	victim	prey	aggressor

W

1	wait	linger	leave
4	wander	stroll about aimlessly	walk purposefully
3	war	conflict	peace
4	ward	adopted person	
3	warehouse	storage building	
2	warm	hot	cold
7	wedge	constrict	release
2	weekend	Saturday and Sunday	weekday
6	welcome	acceptable	unwelcome
4	welfare	social service	
3	well-to-do	rich	poor
2	wet	moist	dry
5	wide	broad	narrow
4	withdraw	retreat	emerge
5	win	get	lose
6	work	labor	rest
1	world	earth	
2	worry	concern	unconcern
3	worse	more unfavorable	better

9	worship	pray	blaspheme
3	wrong	error	right
3	wrong side of the tracks	ill-bred	well-bred

Y

2	yell	shout	whisper
2	young	youthful	old

Index

A

B

C

P

Q

V

Verb phrase, 7

W

Whispers of the Ages, 19, 20
Wisconsin, 153
Words, 199-200